S0-EHE-363

9-4

POPULAR SONG & Youth Today

Books in the YOUTH WORLD Series

POPULAR SONG & YOUTH TODAY

CONTEMPORARY FILM &
THE *NEW* GENERATION

PEACE, WAR & YOUTH

POPULAR SONG & YOUTH TODAY

Edited by
LOUIS M. SAVARY

ASSOCIATION PRESS
New York, N.Y.

Popular Song & Youth Today
Copyright © 1971 by Association Press
291 Broadway, New York, N.Y. 10007

Standard Book Number: 8096-1800-1

Library of Congress Catalog Card Number: 78-129427

Printed in the United States of America

Acknowledgments

Our gratitude goes to the many authors, whose words are the heart of this book, and to their agents and publishers. A special note of thanks is due to Mr. Edward Konick of Charlton Publishing Co. whose issues of *Hit Parader* and *Song Hits* reprint every month scores of lyrics of the latest and best popular songs.

Acknowledgment and copyright notices for song lyrics are given in the text below the individual lyrics. In addition, grateful acknowledgment is made to:

Farrar, Straus & Giroux, Inc. for selections by Tom Wolfe and Phil Spector from Tom Wolfe's *Kandy-Kolored Tangerine-Flake Streamline Baby,* 1967; Grosset & Dunlap, Inc. for selection by Richard Goldstein from *The Poetry of Rock,* 1969; Robert B. Luce, Inc. for selections by Charles Boeckman from *Cool, Hot and Blue,* 1968; The New American Library for selections from *The Rock Story* by Jerry Hopkins. Copyright © 1970 by Jerry Hopkins. Reprinted by arrangement with The New American Library, Inc. New York; by Jerry Garcia from Burton H. Wolfe's *The Hippies,* 1968; G. P. Putnam's Sons for selection by Julius Fast from *The Beatles: The Real Story,* 1968; Random House, Inc. for selection by Jonathan Eisen from *The Age of Rock,* 1969; Stein and Day Publishers for selections by Nik Cohn. Copyright © 1969 by Nik Cohn. From the book *Rock From the Beginning.* Reprinted with permission of Stein and Day Publishers.

Acknowledgment is also gratefully made to the following magazines and newspapers: *The American Scholar* for selection by Ralph J. Gleason; *Cheetah* for selection by Robert Christgau; *Daybreak* for selection by Joan Baez;

Acknowledgment is also gratefully made to the following magazines and newspapers: *The American Scholar* for selection by Ralph J. Gleason; *Cheetah* for selection by Robert Christgau; *Daybreak* for selection by Joan Baez; *Esquire* for selections by Elvis Presley and Stanley Booth; *Evergreen Review* for selections by Nat Hentoff, Paul McCartney and Ringo Starr; Columbia University *Forum* for selections by Joan Peyser and John Lennon; *High Fidelity* for selections by Morgan Ames and Gene Lees; *Hit Parader* for selections by Grace Slick and Jefferson Airplane; *Jazz and Pop* for selections by Frank Kofsky and Frank Zappa; *Life* for selection by Frank Zappa; *The New York Post* for selection by Murray Kempton; *Nova* for selection by Mick Jagger; *Ramparts* for selections by Janis Joplin and Michael Thomas; *Saturday Review* for selections by John Cohen, David Crosby, Burt Korall and Ellen Sander; *Studies on the Left* for selections by Lawrence and Bob Dylan; *Time* for selections by Rudolph Bing and Sheila Wilson; *The Washington Post* for selections by Alan Aldridge and Paul McCartney; World Journal Tribune for selection by James Brown. The selections by Paul Williams and Alfred G. Aronowitz are from articles reprinted in Jonathan Eisen's *The Age of Rock*. The selection from Leonard Bernstein is from his CBS-TV Special on rock music.

Photo credits

Gerald Becker 107; Leslie Becker 24, 29, 137; Laurence B. Fink 10, 35, 49, 55, 64, 88, 94, 102, 111, 133, 154; Cynthia Grey 17, 76; Ettie de Laczay 68, 79; Shelly Rusten 22, 27, 30, 39, 45, 53, 83, 115, 126, 129, 134; David Sagarin 84, 152.

CONTENTS

Prologue

If you were drunk,
and you were out there
dancing and sweating
and really *feeling* the music
(every muscle & fiber
of your being, etc., etc.)
and the music suddenly
got louder and more vicious . . .
louder and more viciouser
than you could ever imagine
(and you danced harder
and got sweaty and feverish)
and got your unsuspecting self
worked up into a total frenzy,
bordering on electric Buddha nirvana
total acid freak cosmic integration
(one with the universe),
and you were drunk & hot
& not really in control of your body
or your senses
(you are possessed by the music),

and all of a sudden the music
gets EVEN LOUDER . . .
and not only that:
IT GETS FASTER & YOU CAN'T BREATHE
But you can't stop either;
it's impossible to stop
and you know that you can't black out
because it feels too good . . .
I ask you now,
if you were drunk
and all this stuff is happening
all over the place
and somebody
(with all the best intentions in the world)
MADE YOU STOP
so he could ask you this question:
"Is a force this powerful to be overlooked
by a society that needs
all the friends it can get?"
Would you listen?

Frank Zappa

Introduction

In the *popular* music of the forties and early fifties, romance and innocence and escape were universal themes. Cole Porter sketched scenes that evoked a glittering high society with candlelight and champagne. Richard Rodgers and Oscar Hammerstein created a Bali H'ai that whispered, on the wind of the sea, "Come to me." Hoagy Carmichael wrote of magic nights, moon mists, and dreams of long ago.

But in the past few years, something new has been happening in popular music. Simon and Garfunkel songs tell of the troubled waters, the sounds of silence, and the communications barriers among people. John Sebastian, formerly of the Lovin' Spoonful, fills his music with the drumming din of a pneumatic hammer to suggest a heavy, humid city, with love in sweat and shadow. Bob Dylan sings of passports and riot squads, of burning cigarettes and sniffing glue, of neighborhood threats and an old-fashioned big brass bed.

In many ways the popular records sold today are a mirror of the contemporary young Americans who buy them. The typical song speaks of a world that wants to be open to life; yet it finds that world complex and confusing, filled with contradictions. Young people in the United States and Canada—and in the rest of the world, too—

somehow fuse these contradictions in their personalities. So do the songwriters, like the Beatles. Or like Bob Dylan, in this interview in *Rolling Stone:*

Interviewer: Many people—writers, college students, college writers—all felt tremendously affected by your music and what you're saying in the lyrics.

Dylan: Did they?

Interviewer: Sure. They felt it had a particular relevance to their lives . . . I mean, you must be aware of the way that people come on to you.

Dylan: Not entirely. Why don't you explain it to me?

Interviewer: I guess if you reduce it to its simplest terms, the expectation of your audience—the portion of your audience that I'm familiar with—feels that you have the answer.

Dylan: What answer?

The songwriters and the young people today hate phoniness, and yet they may sometimes find themselves cheating. They are hungry for knowledge and information yet often sick of school. They value supremely their and their friends' personalities—while they discard as of no value someone they find false.

Young people today are at once cruel and kind, obsessed with speed yet exhausted by pressures, fascinated with thrills but frightened at death. They prize the "tough," yet hunger for gentleness. They strive to be "cool," yet search for intimacy.

Some critics have strong reservations about the effects of popular song on young people. For example, John Cohen writes:

> Topical songs are like newspapers; pertinent to the latest developments, bearing the latest ideas, and ending up in the garbage can . . . for young people in the cities, the topical songs have become abstract emotional substitutes for what is going on in the world; and although this can be a good factor when it stimulates people to action, more often it is a delusion . . . topical songs blind young people into believing they are accomplishing something in their own protest, when, in fact, they are doing nothing but going to concerts, record stores, and parties at home.

But whether or not young people grasp the significance of their music, the lyrics of popular music today do search for meaning. More than ever before, songs deal with concrete personal values. In them there is little of the romantic and sentimental. Most popular music of the young today is specific, hard-nosed and realistic–and very serious about human and social problems. Too serious, maybe. Today "color radio" broadcasts songs with lyrics about divorce, drugs, and death. Pop records spin themes of self-reflection, alienation and revolt. Lyrics tell of loneliness and despair, of insanity and defiance. In short, contemporary popular music reaches out to all kinds of life experiences.

The narratives in certain popular songs of today are sometimes shudderingly realistic, dealing with death and murder, destruction and violence. They are reminiscent of the tone of the 16th century ballad, the blood-curdling "Lord Randal:"

"O where hae ye been, Lord Randal, my son?
O where hae ye been, my handsome young man?"
"I hae been to the wild wood; mother, make my bed soon,
For I'm weary wi hunting, and fain wald lie down."

"Where gat ye your dinner, Lord Randal, my son?
Where gat ye your dinner, my handsome young man?"
"I dined wi my true-love; mother, make my bed soon,
For I'm weary wi hunting and fain wald lie down."

"What gat ye to your dinner, Lord Randal, my son?
What gat ye to your dinner, my handsome young man?"
"I gat eels boiled in broo; mother, make my bed soon,
For I'm weary wi hunting, and fain wald lie down."

"What became of your bloodhounds, Lord Randal, my son?
What became of your bloodhounds, my handsome
young man?"
"O they swelled and they died; mother, make my bed soon,
For I'm weary wi hunting and fain wald lie down."

"O I fear ye are poisoned, Lord Randal, my son!
O I fear ye are poisoned, my handsome young man!"

"O yes! I am poisoned; mother, make my bed soon,
For I'm sick at the heart, and I fain wald lie down."

"Lord Randal," like some pop music today, is a folk song. It is also a ballad–with a narrative progression, like Bobbie Gentry's "Ode to Billy Joe" or Miller and McCoy's "Got to See if I Can't Get Mommy." It is a kind of gothic horror story, and a bit surrealistic–as some Beatles songs and other contemporary songs are. An updated version of "Lord Randal" has in fact appeared in an album by The Incredible String Band. In "Pictures in a Mirror" they sing of Lord Randal in jail unfolding the events of his macabre story.

"Lord Randal," the sixteenth-century ballad, also qualifies as poetry–as would some compositions of Paul Simon of Simon and Garfunkel (who draws on ancient poetic tradition for songs like "Scarborough Fair") and Bob Dylan and Leonard Cohen and Robin Williamson and many others. Today's song lyrics often have intrinsic literary value, and therefore a quality of poetic permanence.

In its content, today's popular music as a whole also offers the listener a selection of values, of ways of living, behaving and reacting. Unlike the popular songs of yesterday, today's music is not merely selling sentimental, sweet romance and easy escape. It has accepted a larger task. It is expected to comment on personal values, to confront problems in human relations, to speak out on human injustice, to explore loneliness, to struggle with desperation and alienation, to unite those who wish to reform the institutions of society.

Generally speaking, then, popular songwriters today recognize that they have a responsibility. They may not always act on it. They may sometimes be arrogant and unthinking, but often enough the responsibility is accepted. Many of the songwriters and songs discussed in this book reflect and face very specific problems of human value and purpose.

The meanings of the words and music in popular song are intimately connected with the writers who composed them and the artists who perform them. These meanings have matured with the growth of this new kind of top-forty music during the past decade. The short history of rock presented in the first chapter serves as a setting and introduction to the study of themes and values in the later chapters.

Part 1

A SHORT HISTORY OF THE MEANING OF ROCK ITS PERFORMERS AND ITS AUDIENCE

In April 1954, an aging country 'n' western singer called Bill Haley made a record called "Rock Around the Clock." By 1955 it was a hit in America, and then it was a hit in Britain, and then it was a hit all over the world. And it just kept on selling; it wouldn't quit. It stayed on the charts for one solid year.

By the time it was finished, it had sold fifteen million copies. It had also started rock.

Nik Cohn

Gonna rock it up right tonight . . .

Julius Dixon
"Teenage Meeting"

This was, truly, a new generation—the first in America raised with music constantly in its ear, weaned on a transistor radio, involved with songs from its earliest moment of memory.

Ralph J. Gleason

2
FRANKS

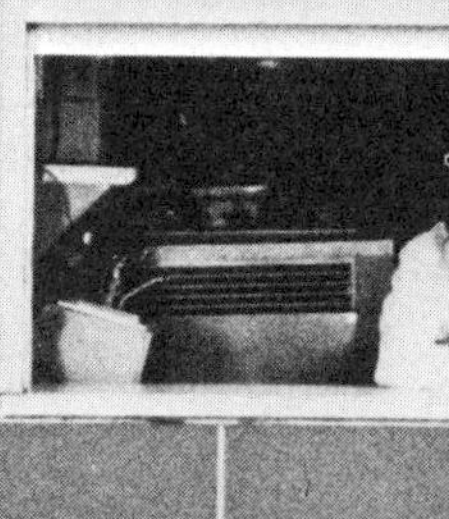

In 1956, just one year following the release of "Rock Around the Clock," the first rock 'n' roll coronation was held, and the undisputed king was Elvis Aaron Presley, then just old enough to vote.

Jerry Hopkins

I just want to tell y'awl not to worry—them people in New York and Hollywood are not gone change me none.

Elvis Presley
July 4, 1956

Reluctantly, almost unwillingly, show business accepted Elvis. Ed Sullivan, who only a couple of months before had condemned Presley as being "unfit for a family audience," now was obliged to pay him $50,000 for three brief appearances. However, Elvis was photographed only from the waist up . . .

Stanley Booth

"Mama, do you think I'm vulgar on the stage?"

"Son, you're not vulgar, but you're puttin' too much into your singin'. Keep that up and you won't live to be thirty."

"I can't help it, Mama. I just have to jump around when I sing. But it ain't vulgar. It's just the way I feel. I don't feel sexy when I'm singin'. If that was true, I'd be in some kinda institution as some kinda sex maniac."

Elvis Presley

All around the world, rock and roll is all they play . . .

Robert Blackwell
"All Around the World"

In 1956 The Encyclopaedia Britannica *yearbook called rock 'n' roll "insistent savagery."*

Don't Step on My Blue Suede Shoes

Elvis Presley

All day long you've been waiting to dance . . .

Chuck Berry
"School Day"

Where the sound is so loud that conversation is impossible, the hypnotic beat works a strange magic. Many dancers become literally transported. They drift away from their partners; inhibitions flake away, eyes glaze over, until suddenly they are seemingly swimming alone in a sea of sound.

TIME

Man now expresses himself through song and dance as the member of a higher community; he has forgotten how to walk, how to speak and is on the brink of taking wing as he dances . . . no longer the artist, *he has himself become* a work of art.

Friedrich Nietzsche

I give everything that is in me. And when I get going, I'm gone. It's the only time I feel whole.

Sheila Wilson

It is not music to listen to, but music to move to. Rock 'n' roll is our modern version of rituals that have existed in other societies as far back as the time when primitive man shuffled and stomped around a drummer pounding on a hollow log until he fell in a state of mystic frenzy.

Charles Boeckman

Do you, do you, do you, do you wanna dance? . . .

Bobby Freeman
"Do You Wanna Dance?"

I'm a teenage singer, made me a record . . .

Johnny Brandon
"Please Buy My Record"

Let's do the Twist, baby . . .

Chubby Checker

1960 was probably the worst year that rock has been through. Everyone had gone to the moon. Elvis had been penned off in the army and came back to appall us with ballads; Little Richard had got religion, Chuck Berry was in jail, Buddy Holly was dead. Very soon, Eddie Cochran was killed in his car crash. It was a wholesale plague, a wipe-out.

Nik Cohn

In the spring of 1960 the Beatles, in their first significant club engagement, discovered the value of noise.

Joan Peyser

Sound-pressure levels are measured in decibels, named after Alexander Graham Bell. Here are some decibel readings for various sounds:

Breathing	*10 db*
Whisper	*20*
Low street noise	*40–50*
Conversation	*60–70*
Rush-hour traffic, New York	*81*
Food blender	*93*
Pneumatic jackhammer	*94*
Automobile in tunnel	*99*
Subway train rounding curve	*104*
Loud power mower	*107*
Loud motorcycle	*111*
Machine gun	*130*
Jet plane at take-off	*150*
Jet rocket launching	*175*

For long-term exposure to any sound of 85 decibels or above, the U.S. Air Force recommends use of ear protectors to prevent hearing loss.

Millicent Brower

"Why do you have to play so loud?"

"Because it doesn't sound right otherwise."

What was new about it was its aggression, its sexuality, its sheer noise; and most of this came from its beat. This was beat, bigger and louder than any beat before it, simply because it was amplified. Mostly, pop boiled down to electric guitars.

Nik Cohn

I got me a guitar a year ago
Learned how to play in a day or so . . .

Bobby Bare
"The All-American Boy"

We're working with dynamics now. We've spent two years with loud, and we've spent six months with deafening.

Jerry Garcia

I conducted a little poll the other day . . . I started asking kids why they liked rock music. Kids starting about eight years old and running into the middle twenties. Nine out of ten said, "It makes me feel good."

Jerry Hopkins

To begin with, rock 'n' roll is the music teen-agers identify with. It belongs to them. It's their music. In its heavy, driving, all-encompassing beat, they find an outlet for the frustrations and aggressions of a world that grows more complex and confining every day, a world where there are fewer and fewer outlets for teen-age energy and enthusiasm.

Charles Boeckman

People try to put us down
Just because we get around . . .

Peter Townshend
"My Generation"

I get a little angry when people say it's bad music. This music has a spontaneity that doesn't exist in any other kind of music, and it's what is here now. It's unfair to classify it as rock-'n'-roll and condemn it. It has limited chord changes, and some people are always saying the words are banal and why doesn't anybody write lyrics like Cole Porter any more, but we don't have any Presidents like Lincoln any more, either. You know? Actually, it's more like the blues. It's pop blues. I feel it's very American. It's very today. *It's what people respond to today. It's not just the kids. I hear cabdrivers, everybody, listening to it.*

Phil Spector

The new style [of music] quietly insinuates itself into manners and customs and from there it issues a greater force . . . goes on to attack laws and constitutions, displaying the utmost impudence, until it ends by overthrowing everything, both in public and in private.

Plato

Right up through the concrete . . .

Jerry Leiber and Phil Spector
"Spanish Harlem"

Spector, while still in his teens, seemed to comprehend the prole vitality of rock-'n'-roll that has made it the kind of darling holy beast of intellectuals in the United States, England, and France. Intellectuals, generally, no longer take jazz seriously. Monk, Mingus, Ferguson—it has all been left to little executive trainees with their first apartment and a mahogany African mask from the free-port shop in Haiti and a hi-fi. But rock 'n' roll! Poor old arteriosclerotic lawyers with pocky layers of fat over their ribs are out there right now twisting clumsily to rock 'n' roll. Their wives wear stretch pants to the seafood shop. A style of life!

Tom Wolfe

At other periods in history most composers were composer-performers — and many of them were "kids." After all, Haydn had composed his first Mass by the time he was twenty, Mendelssohn had written his Octet for Strings by the time he was sixteen, Schubert was dead at thirty-one—and no one needs reminding of the incredible young Mozart. And closer to our own day, Stan Getz recorded his first great solos when he was seventeen, Woody Herman headed his first band when he was little more than twenty, Duke Ellington had his first band before he was twenty. Artie Shaw, Gerry Mulligan, Ella Fitzgerald were professionals in their teens. Both Kern and Gershwin (whose first song was published when he was eighteen) had written Broadway shows before they were twenty-five. Cole Porter was a comparatively old man when he had his first Broadway hit—twenty-seven. As musicologist Henry Pleasants put it, "Music seems to be largely a young man's art. It has something to do with being in love."

Gene Lees

The popular music scene today is unlike any scene I can think of in the history of all music. It's completely of, by, and for the kids, and by kids I mean anyone from eight years old to twenty-five. They write the songs, they sing them, own them, record them. They also buy the records, create the market, and they set the fashion in the music, in dress, in dance, in hair style, lingo, social attitudes.

Leonard Bernstein

Got no deeds to do,
No promises to keep . . .

Paul Simon
"The 59th Street Bridge Song (Feelin' Groovy)"

It's only me pursuing something I'm not sure of . . .

Bob Lind
"Elusive Butterfly"

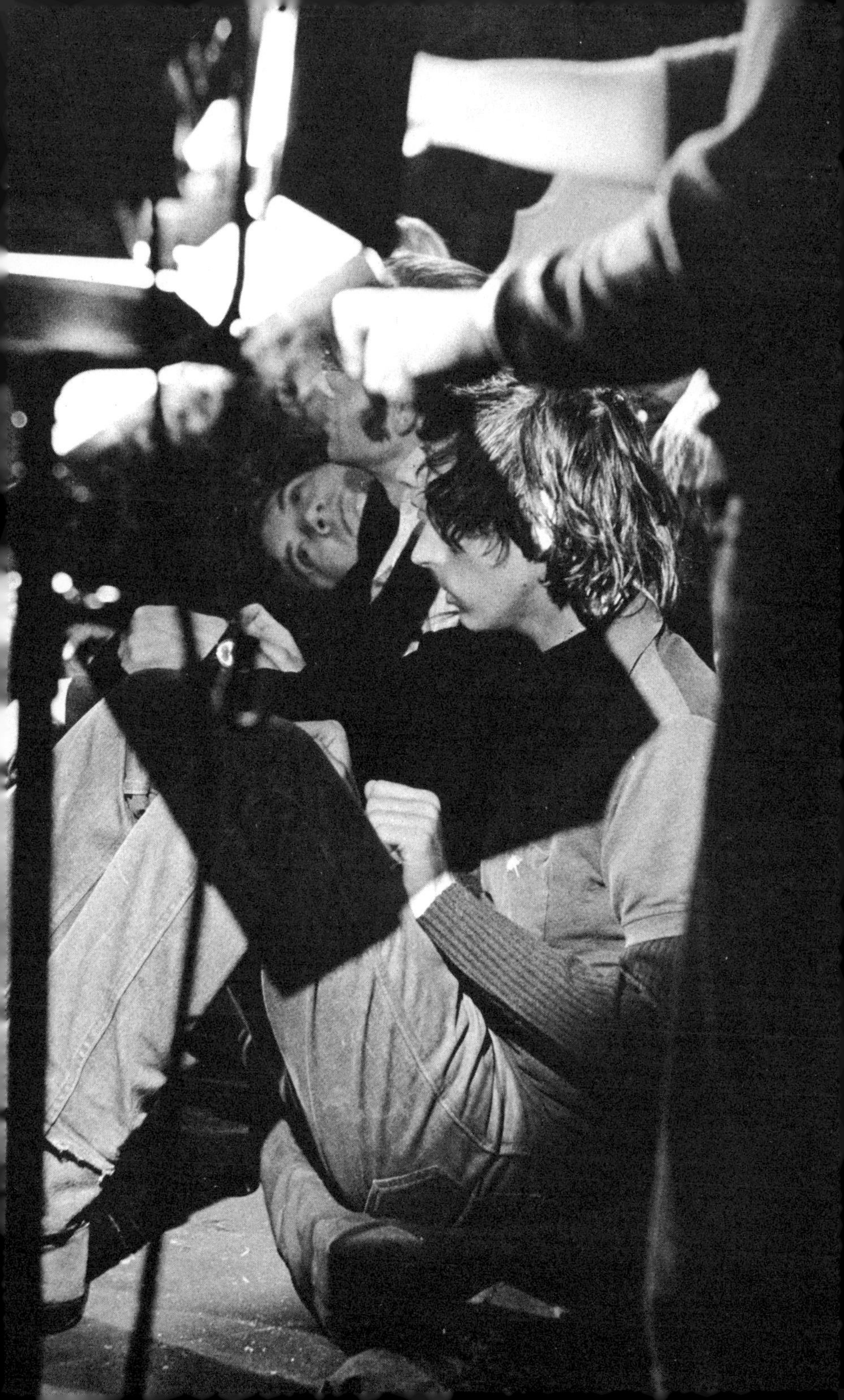

Many people ask what are Beatles? Why Beatles? Ugh, Beatles? How did the name arrive? So we will tell you. It came in a vision—a man appeared on a flaming pie and said unto them, "From this day on you are Beatles with an 'A'." Thank you, Mr. Man, they said, thanking him.

And so they were Beatles.

John Lennon

On Friday, February 7, 1964, the U.S.A. foresaw another crisis with Cuba: Castro had cut off the Guantanamo water supply. . . . London and Paris agreed to build a rail tunnel under the English Channel, an almost dreamlike feat of engineering, while in Jackson, Mississippi, the case against the accused killer of black civil rights leader Medgar Evers went to an all-white jury. . . . And that same day, at Kennedy International Airport in Queens, New York, three thousand teen-agers stood four deep in the upper arcade of the International Arrivals Building to give a screaming, hysterical welcome to four English boys. Airport officials termed the reception "Incredible. We've never seen anything like this before, not even for kings and queens."

Julius Fast

I want to hold your hand . . .

The Beatles

When the "fab four from Liverpool" appeared on The Ed Sullivan Show, *an astonishing seventy-three million people were watching—nearly 45 per cent of the entire population—and the next day* The Washington Post *said in its columns: "Don't knock the Beatles; during the hour when they were on Ed Sullivan's show, there wasn't a hubcap stolen anywhere in America." Even evangelist Billy Graham said he'd violated his rule and watched television on the Sabbath, just to see them.*

Jerry Hopkins

A thousand years ago small groups of uncultivated, bizarrely dressed, oddly named musicians traveled from town to town, singing and accompanying themselves on the vielle. The most famous of these —Jumping Hare, Little String, Ladies Praiser and Rainbow—were rewarded with such fame and luxury that they were imitated by hordes of less gifted, envious men. During the late Middle Ages chronicles refer to "large armies of minstrels," the better ones playing for nobility while lesser troupes entertained at peasant celebrations. Despite the demand for their performances at all levels of society, these itinerant poet-musicians were held in contempt throughout the era. The animus stemmed principally from the Church, which held that their obvious secular joie de vivre *posed a threat to the spiritual welfare of its people.*

Joan Peyser

The police formed cordons. Then the car door opened and the Rolling Stones got out, all five of them . . . and they weren't real. They had hair down past their shoulders, and they wore clothes of every color imaginable, and they looked mean, they looked just impossibly evil.

In this gray street, they shone like sun gods. They didn't seem human: they were like creatures off another planet, impossible to reach or understand, but most exotic, most beautiful in their ugliness.

They crossed toward the stage door, and this was the chance the girls had been waiting for, so they began to surge and scream and clutch. But then they stopped, they just froze. The Stones stared straight ahead, didn't twitch once, and the girls only gaped. Almost as if the Stones weren't touchable, as if they were protected by some invisible metal ring. So they moved on and disappeared. And the girls went limp behind them and were quiet. After a few seconds, some of them began to cry.

Nik Cohn

Of course I do occasionally arouse primaeval instincts, but I mean, most men can do that. They can't do it to so many. I just happen to be able to do it to several thousand people. It's fun to do that. It's really just a game, isn't it? I mean these girls do it to themselves. They're all charged up. It's a dialogue of energy. They give you a lot of energy and take a lot away. Maybe they want something from life, from me. Maybe they think I can give it to them. I don't know.

Mick Jagger

"What's it all mean?"
"The answer, my friend, is blowin' in the wind . . ."

Bob Dylan

Right then, pop began to be something more than simple auto-noise; it developed pretensions, turned into an art form, a religion even, and in all of this, Dylan was the mover.

Nik Cohn

Certainly, the teenagers thrill, overtly and sexually, to their demigods, their heroes. But as they move away from the passion of the dance hall and the rock concert, they seem to be moving into greater independence, not greater dependence on charismatic figures. The people they venerate are those like Bob Dylan, who is less liked for his pelvic contortions than for the poignancy and poetry of his songs, and for what is seen as his genuine ability to speak to the needs of a generation alienated from technological, manipulative society.

Jonathan Eisen

As for rock 'n' roll itself, one could say it is music older than jazz. The history of jazz goes back some sixty or seventy years. The history of the steady simple beat is as old as mankind. When the dancer loses himself completely in this throbbing pulse, his consciousness becomes blurred and he is hardly aware of the music.

Charles Boeckman

Every period which abounded in folk songs has, by the same token, been deeply stirred by Dionysiac currents.

Friedrich Nietzsche

Once more he stept into the street,
    And to his lips again
Laid his long pipe of smooth straight cane;
    And ere he blew three notes (such sweet
Soft notes as yet musician's cunning
    Never gave the enraptured air)
There was a rustling, that seemed like a bustling
    Of merry crowds justling at pitching and hustling,
Small feet were pattering, wooden shoes clattering,
    Little hands clapping and little tongues chattering,
And, like fowls in a farm-yard when barley is scattering,
    Out came the children running.
All the little boys and girls,
    With rosy cheeks and flaxen curls,
And sparkling eyes and teeth like pearls,
    Tripping and skipping, ran merrily after
The wonderful music with shouting and laughter.

Robert Browning
from *The Pied Piper of Hamelin*

Bob Dylan was strange. Technically, he was nothing at all: he played bad guitar and blew bad mouth organ. He hardly even sang in tune, and his voice was ugly; it came through his nose and whined. Still, it was oddly mesmeric; it wriggled inside your head. Even when you didn't like it, it bruised you.

Nik Cohn

Dylan had found his proper milieu. The corduroy cap, the dungarees, the deliberately ungrammatical language, the "folk" spelling of words like "the," the mannerisms, the consciously simplistic stance and the way in which Dylan protested against injustice were all symptoms. They reflected a deep-seated drive of Dylan's, the will to make himself into a type: the vagabond folk-poet of the thirties, the hungry, restless, freedom-loving friend and comrade of the oppressed. Many of the younger Village folk enthusiasts who formed his earliest admiration society were responding to this image, this persona of Dylan's rather than to his singing or to his harmonica playing. It was not until his second record, The Freewheelin' Bob Dylan, *which, unlike his first record, presented him not simply as a singer but as a folk bard, that Dylan began to acquire a large following . . . Dylan became very popular only when people began treating him as a seer as well as a singer.*

Lawrence Goldman

"If I ran the zoo,"
Said young Gerald McGrew,
"I'd make a few changes,
That's what I'd do."

Dr. Seuss

You can't mess with people's heads, that's for sure. But that's what music's all about, messing with people's heads.

Jimi Hendrix

Forms and rhythms in music are never changed without producing changes in the most important political forms and ways.

Plato said that.

There's something happenin' here. What it is ain't exactly clear. There's a man with a gun over there tellin' me I've got to beware. I think it's time we STOP, children, what's that sound? Everybody look what's goin' down.

The Buffalo Springfield said that.

For the reality of politics, we must go to the poets, not the politicians.

Norman O. Brown said that.

For the reality of what's happening today in America, we must go to rock-'n'-roll, to popular music.

I said that.

Ralph J. Gleason

I think that pop musicians in today's generation are in a fantastic position—they could rule the world, man.

Graham Nash

On January 25, 1967, a building collapsed in mid-town Manhattan. Spectators gathered, disaster being one of New York's favorite forms of entertainment. Among the passers-by at the moment was a serious-looking young man looking for a path through the people. "There's Paul Simon!" exclaimed a young office girl. The focus of the crowd shifted quickly from the accident to the young man, who lowered his head, braced his shoulders, and hurried around the corner.

Morgan Ames

Paul Simon's lyrics are the purest, highest, and most finely wrought kitsch of our time. The lyrics I've been putting down are not necessarily easy to write —bad poetry is often carefully worked, the difference being that it's easier to perceive flaccidly—but the labor that must go into one of Simon's songs is of another order of magnitude. Melodies, harmonies, arrangements are scrupulously fitted. Each song is perfect. And says nothing . . . Like Kahlil Gibran all he's really doing is scratching them where they itch, providing some temporary relief but coming nowhere near the root of the problem. Simon's content isn't modern, it is merely fashionable, and his form never jars the sensibilities.

Robert Christgau

To sing is to love and to affirm, to fly and to soar, to coast into the hearts of the people who listen, to tell them that life is to live, that love is there, that nothing is a promise, but that beauty exists, and must be hunted for and found.

Joan Baez

In San Francisco, we play for free in the park. You can't find a better audience than that, they're beautiful.

Janis Joplin

Now the band was ragged, the music was manic, overblown, most of the time incoherent, they played fast and loud but nothing much went anywhere, it was an anarchic, psychedelic jerk-off. But Janis something was, truly, something else. She was so tough. She sang like a rock-and-roll banshee and leaped about the stage like a dervish. It was the raunchiest, grittiest, most attacking rhythm-and-blues singing I'd ever heard, it made the fifteen-year-old kid next to me feel so good he spilled a bottle of orange Day Glo all over my shoes.

"Who's that," I asked him.

"Oh, it's Janis Joplin," he said. "Look at your shoes."

Michael Thomas

It can be pretty scary up where I am. I mean like everybody's watching. Know what I mean? The whole world. Black and white. I'm carrying the whole thing. Right now, in what I'm doin', I'm doin' more for the Negro cause than any of them other *cats. I'm talkin' about* Soul. *Forgettin' that other stuff. That's silly. I'm talkin' about bein'* alive, *man. About* feelin'.

I am one of the most alonest guys. You hip to that? Like I'm a very serious person. Know what I mean? I've got a lot *of problems. I'm real* confused, *you know. But I gotta keep it all to myself. All inside me. 'Cause there ain't no one I can really talk to. Not* really talk. *You dig? . . .*

I gotta be hip to what's goin' on all the time. Know what I mean? When you write songs it's the same with doin' anything creative. You gotta be able to reach *people. So it ain't enough just to know all there is about any one special thing. Like music. You gotta be diggin'* everything that's happening. *You gotta be* at least *eighty-five per cent up on everything. And you gotta try for one hundred per cent.*

James Brown

Somewhere along the line the word soul *got used, sounded right, and stuck. In no time it had become the most overused cliché in the whole range of popular music. It has stayed that way ever since.*

Nik Cohn

The real artists are mainly colored artists. I never did like the Perry Comos or the Sinatras. I don't buy that kind of art. If whites sang like the coloreds did, I'd buy their records.

Ringo Starr

At a recent Crosby, Stills, Nash, and Young concert in New York, Graham Nash introduced "Carry On" in a snide tone of voice as "a little ray of hope for you-all." Stephen Stills, who wrote the song, flashed a peace sign with an unmistakably sarcastic grimace. Neil Young just stood there in skinny patched jeans and looked forlorn. The concert was an uphill climb that didn't quite make it. The group played to an hysterical audience of young urban inmates with nothing to applaud but their own unfounded enthusiasm, and they gave riotous standing ovations to the embarrassed astonishment of the group. Are the young audiences less selective these days? No, just a little more desperate than usual.

Ellen Sander

We're going through the same things that they are. It's getting harder and harder to make happy music.

David Crosby

When I find myself in time of trouble, it's not the swashbuckling city-bred rock 'n' roll I seek; it's the gentle minstrelsy and blues wafting from across the Atlantic or in from the hinterlands, where folks are not in so much torment, that reaches and moves me.

Ellen Sander

Bean Blossom, Indiana: The Fourth Annual Blue-grass Festival

There was a good fellowship among leather-faced men in Western garb, teenage groupies posturing around the musicians, long-haired hippies with their no-bra chicks and red-neck farmers with their wives sprawled in lawn chairs and print dresses. "The people bring me to Bean Blossom," a 24-year-old jazz pianist from Chicago named Bob Hoban told Newsweek's *Bernice Buresh. "It's so relaxing that you can carry yourself home in a bucket when you leave here."*

NEWSWEEK

The times they are a-changin' . . .

Bob Dylan

A rock-opera at the Met

I didn't understand a thing about Tommy *myself, but then I don't understand everything about* Don Giovanni *either.*

Rudolf Bing

And the beat goes on . . .

Sonny Bono

Part 2

SOME THEMES IN POPULAR SONG TODAY

1 IMAGES OF Man and Woman

Twenty or thirty years ago, everything was simple and clear, as far as popular song was concerned. Man was made for woman, and woman for man. It was the era of *Guys and Dolls*. Frank Loesser wrote "I've Never Been in Love Before," and "Now all at once it's you and you forevermore." It was an age of daydreams and innocence and Broadway was playing musical comedies like *Annie Get Your Gun* and *Oklahoma* and *The King and I* and *Kiss Me Kate* and *Brigadoon*. And at the end, everybody married the one they dreamed of marrying and they lived happily every after. Everyone was insane with love, like the singer in the lines from "Where's Charley?"

> Now all at once you've kissed me
> and there's not a thing I'm sane enough to say
> except, My Darling . . .

In the love songs of earlier decades, sentimental exaggeration was common. Every guy's girl was a goddess and every girl's guy was a hero. Life was an Easter Parade. Love was romantic and mesmerizing; everyone could forget his troubles and "get happy." As long as boy and girl were together, nothing could go wrong. "You look at me and suddenly it's Spring:" Nature itself responded to the beatific power of love and romance. "The moon stood still on Blueberry Hill." And, in "The Serenade of the Bells," love made the broken bells chime again. Love seemed to promise that life together for boy and girl would be one long series of happy miracles to store up for remembering.

Contemporary songs usually deal very differently with the man-woman relationship. One theme is that a satisfying married relationship is made up of simple experiences. Honest and unromantic, "Little Green Apples" maintains that love, if it is real, has no need to exaggerate. "Didn't We," on the other hand, cautions that love is not a simple matter of misty-eyed romance, but an experience that sometimes fails and hurts.

When love failed or met obstacles, according to the older songs, the solution was more love. Some songs today are that way, too. Love and kisses solve all problems. But "Isn't It Lonely" and "Got to See if I Can't Get Mommy" tell of situations that can't be dealt with simply by increased doses of "love."

If girls were goddesses in the songs of an earlier era, the female image has changed–or rather multiplied. Three songs discussed in this chapter–"To Know Him Is To Love Him," "Respect," and "I Walk the Line"–present three different views of today's woman and wife, reflecting the complex social structures of today's society.

LITTLE GREEN APPLES quiet happiness

"Little Green Apples" describes a happy relationship between a husband and wife. There are no extreme statements or exaggerated language. Love is no "Magnificent Obsession." For them life is made up of simple things like saying "hi" or meeting for lunch.

The images of happiness are taken from their own household world, the picture books their children look at and the toys they play with, the weather, green apples and autumn leaves. The song seems to imply that when love is genuine and deep, it finds meaning in all the little things of life.

From the first smile in the morning across the breakfast table, life is natural and unforced, patient and outreaching. This understanding of love that welcomes the children fully into the relationship of man and woman—with images of puppy dogs and BB guns, Mother Goose and Dr. Seuss—seems in conflict with the kind of "Love-that-excites-me-passionately" quite common in other contemporary popular songs, such as "Hey There, Lonely Girl," "Baby, Take Me in Your Arms," or "Whole Lotta Love." In many ways, "Little Green Apples" is far more gentle.

LITTLE GREEN APPLES

by Bobby Russell

And I wake up in the morning with my hair down
In my eyes and she says, "Hi"
And I stumble to the breakfast table
While the kids are going off to school, goodbye.
And she reaches out an' takes my hand
Squeezes it says, "How you feelin' Hon?"
And I look across at smiling lips that warm my heart
And see my morning sun.
And if that's not lovin' me
then all I've got to say,
God didn't make Little Green Apples
And it don't rain in Indianapolis in the summertime,
There's no such thing as Doctor Seuss,
Disneyland and Mother Goose is no nursery rhyme.
God didn't make Little Green Apples
And it don't rain in Indianapolis in the summertime.
And when myself is feelin' low
I think about her face aglow to ease my mind
Sometimes I call her up at home knowing she's busy
And ask if she could get away and meet me
And grab a bite to eat

And she drops what she's doin' and hurries down
To meet me and I'm always late.
But she sits waiting patiently and smiles
When she first sees me 'cause she's made that way.
And if that's not lovin' me
then all I've got to say,
God didn't make Little Green Apples
And it don't snow in Minneapolis when the winter comes,
There's no such thing as make-believe puppy dogs
And autumn leaves and BB guns.
God didn't make Little Green Apples
And it don't rain in Indianapolis in the summertime.
And when myself is feelin' low I think about
Her face aglow to ease my mind
Sometimes I call her up at home knowing she's busy
And ask if she could get away
and meet me and grab a bite to eat
And she drops what she's doin'
and hurries down to meet me
And I'm always late. But she sits
waiting patiently
And smiles when she first sees me
'cause she's made that way.

DIDN'T WE almost . . .

A series of metaphors describe a man and a woman who tried to succeed in a relationship, and *almost* did. "Didn't We" may perhaps also be trying to describe an act of love that was ultimately unsatisfying. In any case, we never know whether or not the couple will have another chance to try to make it.

The lyric has a much wider application to human experience. It deals with situations where all things point to a successful outcome which is almost, but never, achieved. From this viewpoint the man-woman relationship that looked so promising but ultimately failed becomes a symbol which may be applied to many other levels of human experience.

DIDN'T WE

by Jimmy Webb

This time we almost made the pieces fit
didn't we?
This time we almost made some sense of it
didn't we?
This time I had the answer right here in my hand
Then I touched it and it had turned to sand.

This time we almost sang the song in tune
didn't we?
This time we almost made it to the moon
didn't we?
This time we almost made our poem rhyme
This time we almost made that long hard climb
Didn't we almost make it this time.

ISN'T IT LONELY TOGETHER without love

A young couple are on their honeymoon. Instead of being pleasant for them, the honeymoon is a time of sadness and shame. They were married to "take care of" the girl's pregnancy. There seems to be no love between the two; the child she bears was conceived in an act of passion. Hence, the boy and girl feel they are merely living a lie. With this outlook, they have only years of loneliness to look forward to in their life together.

A song with lyrics as detailed and explicit as these could never have been widely distributed a generation ago.

ISN'T IT LONELY TOGETHER

by Ray Stevens

Every day it's easier to see that
you're gonna be a mother,
So here we are honeymoon hotel room
married to each other.
And the smile upon your trembling lips is brave
but it don't cover up those tears you've cried,
And though I'm trying hard all the emptiness I feel is
just too big to hide.
And we've got nothing in common
but our name and our shame
and the blame for letting
passion's foolish flame burn wild,
And now we've got to cover up the fact
with an act to atone for our mistake
and to protect the child,
And we've agreed to try to try and live a lie,
But baby, I think it's all in vain,
We're just not birds of a feather,
Isn't it lonely together?

GOT TO SEE IF I CAN'T GET MOMMY (TO COME BACK HOME) **tragedy**

Like the sixteenth-century ballad "Lord Randal," each stanza of "Got to See" becomes more painful to hear than the one before. It is a story of deepest anguish.

A young couple, poor but deeply in love, get married, borrowing his mother's wedding ring for the ceremony. They begin life in a shack, struggling day after day in poverty. Each of their children is almost torn from the womb, so that mommy can get back to work in the fields. She never complains. Until one day the situation becomes too much for her to bear and she disappears.

The husband, moved by pleas of little Suzie and little Davie, goes off in search of mommy. For he knows that he cannot "hold it together by himself." On his way into town, he finds a crowd of people on the bridge and discovers his wife has drowned. Now he must return to their shack and tell the children, "I can't get your mommy to come back home." How will he explain, he wonders, that "Somebody" has taken it out of his hands.

There is not a shred of happiness in the man's life nor any hint of hope in the song's lyric.

TO KNOW HIM IS TO LOVE HIM
high expectations

Here is the story of a girl who has made a definite choice of the man she loves. In the first verse she sings that she loves him. She makes this very clear. In the second verse she imagines what it would be like to be together with him. It's beautiful. In the final verse, however, there is a note of impatience. We learn that he has not yet come to discover that he and she were "meant" for each other.

In a man-woman relationship, often the two people involved do not share a similar depth of feeling. The "true love" conflict has always been a familiar theme in popular music, yet this Phil Spector lyric is simple, stark, hard and real, and has nothing in it of the wispy, dreamy, soft quality of traditional unrequited-love songs.

For those who would easily classify this song as belonging to the romantic tradition, it may be of interest to note that Spector took the title and refrain of the song from the epitaph on his father's tombstone. In this light, the lines, "Everyone says there'll come a day/ When I'll walk alongside of him," develop an unexpected ambiguity.

TO KNOW HIM IS TO LOVE HIM

by Phil Spector

To know, know, know him
Is to love, love, love him.
Just to see him smile
Makes my life worthwhile.
To know, know, know him
Is to love, love, love him,
And I do.

I'd be good to him
And I'd bring love to him.
Everyone says there'll come a day
When I'll walk alongside of him.
Yes, yes, to know him
Is to love, love, love him,
And I do.

Why can't he see,
How blind can he be?
Someday he'll see
That he was meant for me
To know, know, know him
Is to love, love, love him,
Just to see him smile
Makes my life worthwhile.
To know, know, know him
Is to love, love, love him
And I do.

RESPECT non-negotiable demands

Aretha Franklin's recording of "Respect" is perhaps the best-known version of this Otis Redding song. The theme may be classified as something between a statement about womanly rights and a sermon on sexual reciprocity.

The center of this relationship seems to be one of sexual satisfaction. "Respect" is what she wants when he gets home. "Gimme my propers," "whip it to me, baby," "take care of pleasin' me" is what she asks for. The word "respect" takes on a totally new meaning in the context of this song.

The woman who sings does not demean herself and shower her man with sweet promises of faithfulness and undying love. Instead she makes clear to her "baby" her own strengths–she knows she's "got what he wants"–and her non-negotiable demands: what she wants from him.

Compare the character of the woman in this rhythm-and-blues song with the character of the woman in "To Know Him Is to Love Him." The two have very different ideas about the meaning of the man-woman relationship.

I WALK THE LINE gentleman's agreement

As a third example of the place of a woman in today's popular song treatment of the man-woman relationship, consider Johnny Cash's "I Walk the Line." The scene is neither white pop music nor black soul; it is country-western sound and mentality.

The motivation of the single-minded yet difficult fidelity demanded in this song is quite clear: "Because you're mine," he sings, "I walk the line." It is a half-spoken contract, suggesting a kind of justice reminiscent of the days of the cowboys. He is fully in love with her and keeps his mind on her day and night. The happiness he has known with her is proof to him of the rightness of his love.

However, there is a kind of brooding that hangs over the piece. It is as if behind this declaration of true love lurks a fear of what might happen if his woman became "unworthy" of his love. He demands exclusive rights.

2 IMAGES OF Relating

In the young world where personal relationships have grown in number and complexity and people are more aware of the problems of communicating with each other, there has grown up a genre of music that deals with various experiences of relating.

In contemporary popular song, the interest in relationships covers a broader area than boy-and-girl in love, and deals with other relationships than marriage.

"Traces," which among the songs discussed in this chapter is closest in style to the lyrics of the past, never even hints at romantic love and marriage, even though it is quite nostalgic.

"Norwegian Wood" treats a casual relationship with its essentially fragmentary character and unpredictable behavior.

"You Are the Circus" and "The Tracks of My Tears" deal with the complex problem of a person's public face versus the real inner self-image.

Most unlike anything in popular songs of a generation ago are the contemporary songs that treat relating in an almost theoretical way. The three lyrics–"Walk a Mile," "Easy to be Hard," and "Games People Play"–discuss human relationships in general. These songs are almost essays.

TRACES   a love remembered

The haunting melody of "Traces" underscores the "didn't work out right" theme of the lyric. Caught up in a nostalgic mood, the writer tries to reconstruct his relationship by putting together the "bits and pieces" of things that mark past moments shared together–faded photographs, ticket stubs, rings and ribbons. He carries with him during the night these bits and pieces of memory. The relationship that once existed in simple innocence has vanished. He has left only the traces of love. One of these is a trace of hope that she may return.

NORWEGIAN WOOD room in the bath

This Beatles song is typically rich, tantalizing and "it's time-for-bed" ambiguous. It is another version of the boy-meets-and-fails-to-make-girl story, so often the theme of a rock lyric. The song is filled with suspense and mystery. It ends with a question left unanswered.

He was invited to her room; he sat on the floor, drank some wine, talked with her until 2 A.M., when she announced, "It's time for bed." She went off to her bed, he crawled off to sleep in the bathtub. In the morning she was gone (to work), so he built a fire. End of story.

It would be useful to discuss how well this song reflects the casual relationship among young people today, and the expectations such relationships raise–social, sexual and otherwise. It is interesting, too, to speculate about what life means for this working girl.

(This, by the way, is probably the first pop song which employed the sitar, a musical instrument from the East.)

CHERRY HILL PARK day and night games

Mary Hill was a favorite of the boys who, like her, used to frequent an amusement park. The other girls resented her, because she was always so willing to accommodate the boys, though she often made them wait until after dark before she would play her more "thrilling" games. Then Mary went off and got married and there were no more games.

In an earlier era, the song, if done at all, would have come to a happy romantic ending with her wedding. Instead, the song is sung from the perspective of the boys: For them, Cherry Hill Park will never be the same without Mary Hill.

CHERRY HILL PARK

by Robert Nix and Billy Gilmore

Mary Hill used to hang out in Cherry Hill Park.
The games she played lasted all day till way after dark.
All the girls, they criticized her,
But all the guys just idolized her
'Cause Mary Hill was such a thrill
After dark in Cherry Hill Park.

Mary Hill loved to ride on the merry-go-round.
All the guys got eager eyes watchin' Mary go 'round.
In the daytime Mary Hill was a teaser;
Come the night she was such a pleaser.
Oh, Mary Hill was such a thrill
After dark in Cherry Hill Park.

Mary Hill sure was fun down in Cherry Hill Park,
Playin' games with ev'ryone till 'way after dark.
In Cherry Hill Park, in Cherry Hill Park,
Then one day Mary Hill, she married away.
A man with money said, "Come on, honey,"
And she said, "O-kay."

She went away to play a one-man game
And since that day it ain't been the same,
'Cause Mary Hill was such a thrill
After dark in Cherry Hill Park.

Mary Hill sure was fun down in Cherry Hill Park,
Playin' games with ev'ryone till 'way after dark.
In Cherry Hill Park, in Cherry Hill Park,
In Cherry Hill Park. In Cherry Hill Park.

YOU ARE THE CIRCUS   I am the clown

A girl sings her feelings. She has been taken for granted by the boy she loves. It is not a matter of his loving or hating, but of his "not giving a damn." Her love is simply not returned; she is made a joke of; she becomes his clown, the butt of his laughter. Then comes the catch line: "You don't want me but you refuse to let me go."

The image of the clown is a popular one among young people today, but employing the circus image to describe the friend is a novel twist. Perhaps a better image than the circus could be found to describe the kind of relationship existing between this girl and the person she loved.

THE TRACKS OF MY TEARS in the face of the clown

Again the image of the clown appears. Here the emphasis is on the clown as a real person who is sad, or lonely, or disappointed, but nevertheless puts on a happy face to entertain those around him.

The one thing the clown fears is that the girl he loves will not notice that he is acting the clown: that the funny face is really hiding his true feelings.

His is the problem of trying to communicate a different relating image to different people. He is concerned that the attempt to maintain one kind of relationship (to the social group) might in the end destroy another kind of relationship (to the person he loves).

This problem is made more complex by the fact that the boy is actually "with another girl/ Acting like I'm having fun."

GAMES PEOPLE PLAY **using one another**

This country and western ditty won the Grammy award for the best song of the year in 1969. It was played consistently both on pop and adult radio stations. The award it received was an indication of how popular country and western music had become by 1970 among the general listening audience.

The lyric is an almost theoretical discussion of types of destructive relating patterns among people today. The song title and theme reflect a best-selling book called *Games People Play,* by Dr. Eric Berne, a study of the ways people psychologically manipulate one another. The song draws a moral about just how destructive game-playing can be in the human situation.

GAMES PEOPLE PLAY
by Joe South

Oh, the games people play now,
ev'ry night and ev'ry day, now.
Never meanin' what they say, now.
Never sayin' what they mean.
And they while away the hours
In their ivory towers,
'Til they're covered up with flowers,
In the back of a black limousine.

La, da, da, da, da, da, da.
La, da, da, da, da, da, dee.
Talkin' 'bout you and me.
And the games people play.

Oh, we make one another cry;
Break a heart, then we say goodbye;
Cross our hearts and we hope to die.
That the other was to blame.
Neither one will ever give in.
So, we gaze at an eight by ten,
Thinkin' 'bout the things that might have been
It's a dirty rotten shame.

People walkin' up to you,
Singin' Glory Hallelujah!
and they're try'n to sock it to you.
In the name of the Lord.
They gonna teach you how to meditate;
Read your horoscope, cheat your fate,
And furthermore to hell with hate
Come on get on board.

Look around, tell me what you see
What's happenin' to you and me.
God grant me the serenity,
To remember who I am.
'Cause you're givin' up your sanity
For your pride and your vanity,
Turn your back on humanity.
And don't give a da, da, da, da, da.

ANCE COMPANY
FREE BUS
TO
WELFARE SQUARE

EASY TO BE HARD unanswered questions

"Easy to be Hard" comes from the "American Tribal Love-Rock Musical," *Hair*. The song is filled with questions, unanswered questions, perhaps unanswerable questions. "How can people be so cruel?"

The lyric focuses its attack on someone who seems to display care and concern only for "strangers" or "evil and social injustice"—that is, only for a "cause" or for "people" in the abstract. The test of your concern for others, the song says, comes when you meet a friend in need.

EASY TO BE HARD

by James Rado, Gerome Ragni, Galt MacDermot

How can people be so heartless?
How can people be so cruel?
Easy to be hard, easy to be cold,
"No," especially people who care about strangers
Who care about evil and social injustice
Do you only care about the bleeding crowd?
How about a needing friend?

How can people be so heartless?
How can people be so cruel?
Easy to give in, easy to help out
How can people have no feelings?
You know I'm hung up on you
Hard not to surrender, hard not to be easy
How can people be so heartless?
How can people be so cruel?
Easy to be hard, easy to be cold.

WALK A MILE IN MY SHOES   a new mentality

This Joe South lyric is about sensitivity to one's fellow man. Its message about relating is as perennial as Jesus' Sermon on the Mount; and many of the images in the lyric are, in fact, taken from the Bible.

Though the message is age-old, the approach, explained in the first verse, is fresh. The objective is to enter into another's mentality. The hope is that from this new vantage point, people who had the experience of walking in someone else's shoes would be more aware of the feelings and needs of others.

WALK A MILE IN MY SHOES

by Joe South

If I could be you and you could be me
for just one hour,
If we could find a way to get inside
each other's mind.
If you could see you through my eyes
instead of your ego,
I believe you'd be surprised to see
that you'd been blind.

Walk a Mile in My Shoes,
Walk a Mile in My Shoes,
And before you abuse, criticize and accuse,
Walk a Mile in My Shoes.

Now your whole world you see around you
is just a reflection
And the law of common says
you reap just what you sow.
So unless you've lived a life of perfection
You'd better be careful of every stone
that you should throw.

(Chorus)

And yet we spend the day
throwing stones at one another
'Cause I don't think or wear my hair
the same way you do.
Well I may be common people
but I'm your brother
And when you strike out and try to hurt me
it's a-hurtin' you.

(Chorus)

There are people on reservations
and out in the ghettos
And, brother, there but for the grace of God
go you and I.
If I only had the wings of a little angel
Don't you know I'd fly to the top of the mountain
and then I'd cry.

(Chorus)

3

IMAGES of Alienation

Young people today find their lives a mixture of soaring spirits and dark moods. They fight for causes and ideas and yet are constantly in search of fun and kicks. It is a time for dances, dates and undying friendships, a time of enthusiasm, sensitivity and turmoil. In the struggle to grow and develop and find a place in the world, young people often feel lonely, unloved, left out, forgotten, turned away. No one seems to understand, no one seems to care, no one seems even to be listening. Popular songs today reflect this sense of desperation, failure, alienation.

BANKRUPT
STOCK

A DAY IN THE LIFE disturbed or confident?

To understand the Beatles' "A Day in the Life," we should study it in the context of the entire *Sergeant Pepper* album and in the context of Beatle history.

At first, their music was merely simple and fresh. The complex melody lines (complex for rock 'n' roll, that is) and the subtle lyricism would come later. Initially, there was only good, clean fun, and the message was no more complicated or controversial than "I Want to Hold Your Hand" (the Beatles' first Number One hit in America), so innocent and infectious that everyone (parents included) accepted them immediately.

Jerry Hopkins

Sergeant Pepper's Lonely Hearts Club Band was the Beatles' thirteenth album. Musically, it employed more dissonance than ever before, unconventional phrasing and advanced electronic techniques. As a totality–music and message–the album asks to be listened to as a concert. The opening track simulates the tuning-up sounds of a concert hall with the accompanying hubbub of people in the orchestra and audience. Ringo is Sergeant Pepper, the leader of the band, the lonely outsider, the nonintellectual who gets by "with a little help from my friends."

The second side of the album tells explicitly what the first side is all about–"the people who hide themselves behind a wall of illusion." The songs on this side describe people who face life without drugs. But often these are people with sterile, ritualized lives: the elderly couple, the meter-maid, the ordinary man going through an ordinary day with "Nothing to say but what a day/ How's your boy been . . ."

Sergeant Pepper's theme comes back and drives home the hard-to-swallow truth of his inner life. Four times they repeat, "Sergeant Pepper's lonely."

The Beatles affirm in this album, as Joan Peyser says, "the philosophy that Eugene O'Neill expressed in 'The Iceman Cometh'–that man cannot live without illusion."

But the Beatles go one step further in "A Day in the Life." They suggest that if man cannot live without illusion, he cannot live with it either. Here the Beatles express the ultimate realization of the *anomie* of contemporary man. *Newsweek* called it a "Waste Land."

The lyrics are manifestly poetic. But if taken simply as a poetic statement of contemporary despair, the lyric is traditional and deeply so. Many of the images are reminiscent of T. S. Eliot, especially his "Love Song of J. Alfred Prufrock." They are stated strongly, clearly and effectively.

In "A Day in the Life" the singer tells how he had read the daily paper and seen the photo of a man who had "made the grade" but died in a freak auto accident. And he just *had* to laugh. Next, the singer goes to a war film; he *had* to see it, because he had read the book. Then he explains how his life is made up of coffee cups, combs, hat and coat, running for the bus, smoking a cigarette. Finally he describes people as "holes" and he learns that someone has counted how many holes it takes "to fill the Albert Hall."

Lennon's voice says to the audience, as a kind of comment, "I'd love to turn you on." To one critic his voice is "breaking with sadness," while another claims it sounds "calm and certain." In any case the pivotal significance of the song is this surprise line, and we can ask whether it is a statement of discouragement or desperation or nostalgia or confidence.

On the bottom of the album cover there is a burial plot covered with red flowers that spell BEATLES. Joan Peyser explains that "the original Beatles of the 1950s, joyous and innocent, are dead . . . Sergeant Pepper's Lonely Hearts Club Band is pictured in the center of the cover. Its members are adorned with colorful psychedelic costumes and are devastatingly unsmiling. They are the Beatles of today." [Or yesterday. *Ed.*]

At least that's one opinion.

In employing established poetic concepts . . . the Beatles alert us to "stay tuned for meaning" without destroying the force of their music. And the thrust of "A Day in the Life" is magnified through the most incredible orchestral barrage ever to grace a pop composition. There are shiftless rhythms, assaulting chords, and an unbearable crescendo (performed by full orchestra) followed by soft, sonic hum.

Richard Goldstein

OTHER SINGERS, OTHER MOODS

The blues tradition is one of the ways people in the past expressed the hidden, subtle, hard-to-understand things of the heart.

The blues tradition at its truest carried up from the black South a hard realism about problems and sometimes a strong sense of personal aloneness. This harder blues tradition has had a distinct influence on the alienation songs in contemporary music.

Contemporary popular song talks sometimes with bitterness, of illusion and boredom, as in the Beatles' "A Day in the Life." But song today often talks of anxiety and terror found in normal experiences of life, as in "A Whiter Shade of Pale;" or of quiet desperation in a song like "California Dreamin'."

Other lyrics describe ways in which people struggle to find their way out of a negative setting. "I Am a Child" is a search for a mystical river, while the "Strange Young Girls," "called by the Dove," fervently offer "their youth on an altar of acid."

Nothing exists in a vacuum. Some popular songs are reminiscent of the romantic song tradition. And, in fact, they do treat the theme of love lost. However, each adds its own contemporary twist to the theme.

A WHITER SHADE OF PALE **dislocation and upset**

After hearing this heavy-with-anxiety-and-terror poetic lyric, it is hard to believe that the first big pop hit of the Procol Harum was "Winchester Cathedral."

In "A Whiter Shade," the images of flying ceilings, millers and vestal virgins are often rather difficult to fathom; but for all the intellectualism of the lyric, the reality of the terrible beast within things is clearly felt. We are made to feel the confusion, dislocation and physical upset of the people in the place.

The lyric hints of a "turn on" that is not very pleasurable. It is just after the evoking of the Miller's Tale (from Chaucer's *Canterbury Tales*) that the girl's frightened face turns a whiter shade of pale.

CALIFORNIA DREAMIN' nostalgia?

This song, by John Phillips, was written originally for The Mamas and the Papas. It is a kind of protest at the way things are, but the lyric discloses a bitterness and despair that hardly fits the quiet gentle sound of the melody and music.

Some have interpreted the song as "a charming piece of nostalgia." But such an interpretation leaves some unanswered questions. For example, if warmth means love, and winter means coldness and sterility, what about the preacher (presumably a man of warmth and love) who likes the cold?

The singer could have left his cold and wintry place "if I didn't tell her." We may wonder: What exactly is it that he will (or did) tell her, that keeps him from his "safe and warm" California?

CALIFORNIA DREAMIN'

by John Phillips

All the leaves are brown,
And the sky is grey.
I've been for a walk
On a winter's day.
I'd be safe and warm,
If I was in L.A.
California dreamin'
On such a winter's day.

Stopped into a church
I passed along the way.
Oh, I got down on my knees
And I pretended to pray.
You know, the preacher likes the cold.
He knows I'm gonna stay.
California dreamin'
On such a winter's day.

All the leaves are brown,
And the sky is grey.
I've been for a walk
On a winter's day.
If I didn't tell her,
I could leave today.
California dreamin'
On such a winter's day.
On such a winter's day.

I AM A CHILD dreaming alone

Jackson Browne writes for the Beach Boys. Like Brian Wilson, he is a California dreamer. But Browne prefers to dream alone by a rocky seacoast, while Wilson opts for fun and excitement among the crowds at Disneyland in the afternoon.

Jackson is clear and concise. "I Am a Child" is in a sense the story of every young person who has left home in search of a higher meaning. Yet like many who have gone in search of a new way of living–"looking for water and looking for life"–the writer has found no one who "will show me the river."

Why does the singer call himself a child? After all, his move away from his father's house could be interpreted as an act of independence and maturity.

I AM A CHILD IN THESE HILLS

by Jackson Browne

I am a child in these hills
I am away, I am alone
I am a child in these hills
And looking for water
And looking for water.

Who will show me the river
And ask me my name
There's nobody near me to do that
I have come to these hills
I will come to the river
As I choose to be gone
From the house of my father
I am a child in these hills
I am a child in these hills.

Chased from the gates of the city
By no one who touched me
I am away, I am alone
I am a child in these hills
And looking for water
And looking for life.

Who will show me the river
And ask me my name
There's nobody near me to do that
I have come to these hills
I will come to the river
As I choose to be gone
From the house of my father
I am a child in these hills
I am a child in these hills.

STRANGE YOUNG GIRLS cut off from reality

Among young people, "turning on" with drugs has become quite popular, and is often alluded to in rock music today. Usually the musical treatment involves some kind of code or underground language. Thus songs speak of "getting high" or "eating hash," "Mary," "smoking caterpillar," "losing your head." Many of the lyrics–"Puff the Magic Dragon" was one of the first–borrow themes of softness, magic and color from an older poetic tradition. One example of this kind of magical treatment is Samuel Taylor Coleridge's unfinished dream poem, "Kubla Khan."

The very strange, very unromantic "Strange Young Girls" partly shows the new attitude toward drugs. John Phillips, writing about acid heads on Sunset Strip, pictures them as faithful worshippers in ecstasy, moving in an atmosphere of sadness, madness and innocence. The religious overtones are strong, but the doctrine is that of Orpheus and Narcissus. The strange young girls "called by the Dove," are in a world of "wisdom," but cut off from reality.

The melody of the song is stately and somber–thus confusing, or at least contrasting with, the meaning of the lyric.

STRANGE YOUNG GIRLS

by John Phillips

Strange young girls
Colored with sadness
Eyes of innocence
Hiding their madness
Walking the Strip
Sweet, soft, and placid
Offering their youth
On an altar of acid.

Thinking these kisses
Were sent by the dove
Off on a trip
Accompanied by love
Gentle young girls
Holding hands walking
Wisdom flows childlike
While softly talking.

Colors surround them
Bejewelling their hair
Visions astound them
Demanding their share
Children of Orpheus
Called by the dove
Off on a trip
Accompanied by love.

Thinking each trip
Was sent by the dove
Off on a trip
Accompanied by love.

ONE the loneliest number

This Nilsson song revolves about the numbers "one" and "two." "One" is the loneliest number; then comes the experience of "two," a sad experience with a girl. Finally he insists that, after separation, "one" is loneliest–"much more worse than two."

The singer is roundabout; he never admits that he is lonely, even though the girl has left him. Perhaps he is afraid to apply the word "lonely" directly to himself.

Nilsson very purposefully speaks not of "one" as the loneliest number you'll ever "see" or "know" or even "be," but as "the loneliest number that you'll ever *do*."

NO OTHER

4 IMAGES OF the Ways People Live

The following pages present different images of people and the ways they live. Some songs seem to express satisfaction with the way things are and the ways people live—but these are few. Indeed, they stand in striking contrast to the many songs that express social criticism and dissatisfaction with accepted attitudes. In this context of criticism of society, a contented song such as "Sunday Mornin' " is almost like an island in the midst of an ocean of criticism.

Many songs and films of years ago took class distinctions and racial prejudice for granted. Today's songs rarely do.

Young people today are concerned about society. They are outspoken in their dissatisfaction with it and feel free to criticize it. Popular songs reflect this spirit. "Harper Valley PTA" and "White Houses" attack the smugness of middle-class America. In "Master Jack" the singer symbolizes a black Africa—and a black America, too—that has come of age. "These Are Not My People" points up a conflict in social values, while "Love of the Common People" praises a poor but happy family. "The Yard" treats the problem of living within the threat of violence and destruction, while "Everyday People" touches upon many kinds of conflict among people, and urges human beings to get together.

SUNDAY MORNIN' resting quietly

Some people want to live the way others do and to "do what other people do on Sunday mornin'."

Content to enjoy a cup of coffee or listen to the sounds of those who walk along quiet streets, the author seems to say, "All I want is to rest quietly and comfortably with you on Sunday morning."

Compare what the singer says here ("Everything's alright") to the ironic sarcasm of "Harper Valley PTA" and the social sickness described in "White Houses." Can the conflicting attitudes and meanings found in these three songs exist at the same time and in the same neighborhood?

SUNDAY MORNIN'

by Margo Guryan

Sunday mornin', sun shining from your eyes
Sleepy face smiling into mine
Sunday mornin', lots of time with nothing to do
Lots of time to spend with you on Sunday mornin'
It's so quiet in the streets
We can hear the sound of feet walkin' by
I'll put coffee on to brew, we can have a cup or two
And do what other people do on Sunday mornin'
Sunday mornin' Sunday mornin' Sunday
Sunday, Sunday, Sunday
I love Sunday, Sunday mornin'
Come hold me in your arms, I love you
Everything's alright, everything's alright
everything's alright.

HARPER VALLEY PTA   unbecoming behavior

Young people today despise hypocrisy. Consequently, they find this song sardonically satisfying. It is a story of a young woman accused of behavior unbecoming a resident of Harper Valley, who fights back with facts about the hypocritical ways of some of her accusers.

It might be interesting to compare the accusations leveled at the widow, Mrs. Johnson–wearing a miniskirt, drinking and going around with men–with the accusations she directs at some of the members of the PTA–adultery, seduction, drunkenness–and to discuss how the accusations might be ranked in importance or severity.

The young girl who sings the song is obviously on her mother's side and quite happy to tell us about the day "my mama socked it to the Harper Valley PTA."

WHITE HOUSES social comment

"White Houses," which seems partly modeled on "Little Boxes," begins by drawing a contrast between the middle class and the poor, which probably also applies as between blacks and whites. Its message is expressed as a kind of threat: "You better get straight" is the refrain repeated again and again.

The song does not spend much time talking about "the tumble-down black shacks." Rather it focuses its attack on the "white houses in neat little rows" and the social sickness of the white-housed people, with the minds of their young sampling every pleasure and perversion from pot to voyeurism.

The people in white houses have been warned that what they're doing is wrong, "but they don't give a damn." The consequence of their unconcern will be the appearance of "another life." We are not told what "another life" means. Perhaps it means that the young suburbanites will grow up to turn away from their parents and their past? Or perhaps it means that some group of people from outside will spring up to attack and destroy the people in white houses?

MASTER JACK **thank you very much**

Originally from Africa, "Master Jack" describes a relationship between teacher and learner. The setting is not the classroom, however, but real life. It is a comment on social relationships.

The student has learned well what the master taught him, but he has now come to the point where he'd "like to see the world through my own eyes." There seems to be some hatred simmering underneath: "I thank you very much and know you've been very kind/ But I better move along before you change my mind."

Though the lyric can be read on many levels, it may be interpreted as a negro slave speaking to his white master. It thus becomes a social commentary on the race problem in America as well as in Africa.

THESE ARE NOT MY PEOPLE **blind to reality**

This song seems at first glance to be sung to an upper-class girl, a rich kid. From this viewpoint, the singer is severing connections with the girl, who seems to have been "slumming." But the lyrics may be interpreted in other ways.

For example: Is this a night person talking about the people of the world from which the girl comes, or is it a mocking echo of the girl talking about the night people? In any case, it seems that the girl could never make it in the society of the night people. She lost her cool, she was blind to reality, she is a rebel without a cause, a tiger without claws, living in a cloud.

Or is the rich kid a "he"?

THESE ARE NOT MY PEOPLE
by Joe South

First your mama and your papa sent you
to the finest school.
Never let it be said that their little darling was a fool.
With a credit card and your good name,
You were drawn like a moth to a flame,
To the people of the night
Where you more or less lost your cool.

These are not my people.
These are not my people.
It looks like the end my friend.
Gotta get in the wind my friend.

You had twenty-twenty vision and still you were
walkin' 'round blind.
And whether right or wrong, I still tag along behind.
You rejected reality, you thought I had to set you free,
So it's time to say, you go your way and I'll go mine.
It's been a gas, but I'm gonna have to pass.

(Repeat chorus).

You found yourself naked in a world with
no place to hide.
Then you felt the pulse of your God,
And he had died.
You're a rebel, but you got no cause;
You're a tiger, but you got no claws.
They promised you the world on a string,
but you know they lied.
You said you'd be back in a big Cadillac limousine.
But you know I'm inclined to think it's not the kind
that you mean.
'Cause when you fall down off your cloud,
And you're just another face in the crowd,
They're gonna throw you away like last week's
magazines.
Pretty pals, sociable gals.

EVERYDAY PEOPLE against prejudice

The singer seems to feel that he can be all things to all men, that he can fit in anywhere; it makes no difference what group he's in, he says: "I am everyday people."

The song mentions various kinds of prejudice and alleged reasons for hating other people and hints that such attitudes are groundless and of no help to society. Rather there is a tremendous need for human unity. "We got to live together" is the constant refrain.

Perhaps "Everyday People" is an overly simplistic formulation of a complex problem. When analyzed, the song offers no more concrete and positive recommendation than the vague plea: "We've got to live together." But the plea is made with deep conviction and deserves a hearing, if only for its sincerity.

LOVE OF THE COMMON PEOPLE

fortunate unfortunates

The "Common People" of the title are poor people–a little girl who doesn't have a dress to wear to a party, and a family freezing in the winter cold.

The song says that such unfortunates, because they "live in the love of the common people," are really quite fortunate. They have the family pride, the faithfulness of the mother's love, and the dreams of success that the father "buys" for his children.

In general, the song suggests that the life of the common people is difficult, but the rewards of a setting of "love and warm conversation and plenty of prayer" far outweigh the disadvantages.

LOVE OF THE COMMON PEOPLE

by John Hurley and Ronnie Wilkins

Living on free food tickets.
Waterin' the milk from the hole in the roof
Where the rain came through,
What can you do?

Tears from little sister
Crying 'cause she doesn't have a dress
without a patch for the party to go
Oh, but you know she'll get by.

She is living in the love of the common people;
Smiles from the heart of the family man.
Daddy's gonna buy her a dream to cling to,
Mama's gonna love her just as much as she can, she can.

It's a good thing you don't have bus fare.
It would fall through the hole in your pocket.
And you'd lose it in the snow on the ground,
A-walkin' to town to find a job.
Trying to keep your hands warm but the hole in your shoe
lets the snow come through and the chills to the bone.
Boy you better go home where it's warm where you can.

Live in the love of the common people;
Smiles from the heart of the family man.
Daddy's gonna buy you a dream to cling to,
Mama's gonna love you just as much as she can,
she can.

Living on dreams ain't easy but the closer
the knit the tighter the fit,
And the chills stay away.
You take 'em in stride family pride.
You know that faith is your foundation and with
a whole lot of love and warm conversation and plenty
of prayer making you strong where you belong.

Where you can live in the love of the common people,
Smiles from the heart of the family man.
Daddy's gonna buy you a dream to cling to,
Mama's gonna love you just as much as she can,
she can.

THE YARD WENT ON FOREVER

a doomsday sandwich

Like many of the other songs here, this fascinating Jimmy Webb lyric is filled with social criticism.

The song has three parts. The first part predicts the volcanoes and tornadoes of doomsday. The middle section describes an afternoon, like a thousand other afternoons in the life of a mother–clotheslines, lawn sprinklers, children playing, the smells of supper cooking. It seems that familiar pleasures, like the yard, will go on forever. Yet in the final section, in complete contrast, the motifs of eruption and destruction return. What is Webb's purpose in sandwiching the endless backyard between two slices of doomsday?

THE YARD WENT ON FOREVER

by Jimmy Webb

Is everyone safe?
Has everybody got a place to hide?
Is everybody warm inside?
Hear them singing? All the women of Pompei
Standing with the Kansas City housewives in doorways
In volcanoes and tornadoes on doomsday.

There were houses, there were hoses, there
were sprinklers
On the lawn, there was an ironing board
And she would stand amid her understanding
And ask the children what they'd done at school that day.
And the yard went on forever.
There were blouses, with print roses, checkered shirts
And white levis; there was a frying pan
And she would cook their dreams while
they were dreaming.
And later she would send them out to play.
And the yard went on forever.

Is everybody safe?
Has everybody got a place to hide?
Is everybody warm inside?
Hear them singing? All the women of Bombay
Standing with the Nagasaki housewives in doorways
In eruptions and destructions on doomsday.

5 IMAGES OF the World

While the previous chapter dealt with problems of the human condition and life in the human community, many popular songs deal with the world, the purpose of man's existence, the meaning of peace and war and revolution.

Perhaps another title for this chapter could be "The New Patriotism." In the early years of America's independence, Francis Scott Key wrote of "the land of the free and the home of the brave." The Civil War was viewed as a noble cause—a battle for freedom. And Julia Ward Howe could call her song "The Battle Hymn of the Republic." At the turn of the century, Americans looked at the country they had fought for, won and united; to them it was "America the Beautiful."

In contrast, songs during the world wars were rarely given to ennobling themes. Song writers found it difficult to understand why America became involved. So instead of patriotic songs, they produced only entertaining ditties, morale boosters, propaganda. World War I soldiers were advised to "pack up your troubles in your old kit-bag and smile, smile, smile." In World War II they were encouraged to "Accentuate the positive, eliminate the negative." Men in the military were told in "This is the Army, Mr. Jones," about their lot as soldiers: "You've had your breakfast in bed before, but you won't have it there any more."

America danced to the "G.I. Jive" and girls met boys at "The Stage Door Canteen" after a rally to sell war bonds. People made up their own lyrics to popular songs:

Whistle while you work
Whistle while you work
Mussolini is a meanie,
Hitler is a jerk.

Glen Miller played and the Andrews Sisters sang, to a jitterbug rhythm, songs about dropping bombs in Germany's lap.

War in the '40's was mostly a simple matter of good guys and bad guys. And the objective was to destroy the bad guys. Of course, nobody liked war, because it meant that Americans could be killed. So children, mothers, and sweethearts prayed that the enemy would be destroyed and that the men would come home safely, even if it meant "Comin' in on a Wing and a Prayer."

Today all this has changed. Young people question America's involvement in war, any war. They question the use of violence and force whenever it is employed.

"The Song of the Green Berets" which climbed to the top of the charts was a rather isolated instance: a song with the flavor of old-fashioned patriotism. As far as young people are concerned, the real war for America is not being fought in Vietnam or Laos or Thailand or Cambodia, but in the consciences and minds of the people.

For many young people, a national patriotism is too narrow and confining. Their homeland is the world. The new patriotism tends to favor world brotherhood; yet for some the revolution is focused elsewhere. The blacks, the environmentalists, the hippies and the poor have their own brands of patriotism and their own definitions of revolution. There are many different approaches.

MY COUNTRY a new patriotism

This song, popular in the early '70's, contains a statement of a particular kind of patriotism. The words of this song are those of a black person. "I paid three hundred years or more of slave driving," the singer says.

Not so much defiant as straightforward, he seems to place some trust in the ultimate reasonableness of the white man.

(This Is) MY COUNTRY
by Curtis Mayfield

Some people think we don't have the right
To say it's my country.
Before they give in they'd rather fuss and fight
Than say it's my country.

I paid three hundred years or more
Of slave driving, sweat and welts on my back.
This is my country.
Too many have died in protecting my pride
For me to go second class.
We've survived the hard blow and I want you to know

That you'll face us at last
And I know you will give consideration.
Shall we perish unjust, or live equal as a nation?
This is my country.

But name me any other country you can start as a shoe-shine boy and shake hands with the President . . .

James Brown

WONDERFUL WORLD, BEAUTIFUL PEOPLE
the world in a mess

Jimmy Cliff's song looks at the general state of the world and says: We-could-and-we-should-but-we-don't-but-let's-try-to-do-something-about-it-anyway.

The lyrics survey the world situation and find it a mess: fussing, fighting, cheating, biting, scandalizing, hating.

The images of the song do not describe world-level problems, such as hunger, war, social injustice, and so forth. Rather, the lyric treats problems on the level of individual attitudes and situations that are most likely to occur between neighbors, friends, relatives, and so on.

The song asks everybody to learn to love each other. In 1931 George Gershwin wrote a song called "Love is Sweeping the Country"; the love there described was "billing and cooing like the birdies." This is different from the "love" that "Wonderful World" refers to.

FRIENDSHIP TRAIN **a single brotherhood**

"Friendship Train" reads almost like a speech or a sermon. It attempts to speak to everyone, telling of the precarious situation of the world. Its theme, much like that of "My Country," is "We've got to learn to live with one another." The lyric explicitly recalls other popular song titles such as "Eve of Destruction" and "What the World Needs Now is Love." In such songs, even when they are negative, humanity is envisioned as a single brotherhood or as a single problem. "Friendship Train" while vague, is not negative. The lyric invites people to love and understanding, and to "get aboard." When it seems that people are about to object that the friendship plan is impossible, the lyric tells people to calm down, it assures them that we can do it. All we need are willing hearts, then we'll be able to work it out.

VOLUNTEERS the love revolution

In the late '60's, Jefferson Airplane created a fictional group and called them Volunteers of Amerika. The real Volunteers of America are not revolutionary. They are a religious and philanthropic organization similar to the Salvation Army. (The kicky *k* may have been put into the Jefferson Airplane song to avoid confusion or libel.)

Grace Slick of the Airplane once said in an interview:

> If you have a closed mind, it's difficult for you to express yourself. So any confrontation that you have with people, it usually ends really soon with them getting–really, verbally ripped to shreds. Because they don't have the—they have nothing to draw on. All they know is what they don't want. "I don't want that." They aren't making positives.

The "Volunteers" seem interested in positives, but the lyric certainly doesn't make very concrete suggestions. The kind of "revolution" envisaged in the song is not quite clear. It seems to reject the older generation and its values as without "soul." The present generation, says the lyric, "got no destination to hold," implying that it has its own destination to create.

Jefferson Airplane's first hit single was "Don't You Need Somebody to Love?" Buttons the group had made said "Jefferson Airplane Loves You;" Marty Balin said: "The stage is our bed and the audience is our broad. We're not entertaining, we're making love." Bumper stickers proclaimed: GOD IS LOVE and MAKE LOVE, NOT WAR. The Love Generation was born. Love-Ins were a craze. Young people renounced war, politics, cultural hang-ups, to become affectionate peacemakers.

"What the world needs now is love, sweet love . . ." Jackie DeShannon had sung it in 1965 and the movie "Bob & Carol & Ted & Alice" echoed it in 1970. Now, finally, the world was catching on.

MONSTER injustice, freedom, responsibility

The Steppenwolf, who recorded "Monster," are critical of social injustice and social unconcern. The lyric, full of irony and sarcasm, presents a mixed unhappy history of an America which has in the end become a nation of fat, lazy, jaded, unresponsive and irresponsible people. The theme is "America, where are you now?" Even more fundamental is the problem of national identity: What is America? What does it mean to be an American?

Perhaps the most devastating question put to America by the lyric is: "Don't you care about your sons and daughters?"

But for the reader the most puzzling question may be: What exactly is this "Monster?"

MONSTER

by Jerry Edmonton, John Kay, Nick St. Nicholas

Once the religious, the hunted and weary
Chasing the promise of freedom and hope
Came to this country to build a new vision
Far from the reaches of kingdom and Pope.
Like good Christians some would burn the witches,
Later some bought slaves to gather riches.
But still from near and far to seek
America they came by thousands to court the wild.
But she just patiently smiled,
Then bore a child
To be their spirit and guiding light.
Then once the ties with the crown had been broken,
Westward in saddle and wagon it went.
And till the railroad linked ocean to ocean
Many of the lives which had come to an end.
While we bullied, stole and bought our home land,
We began the slaughter of the red man
(Repeat chorus).

The blue and grey they stomped it,
They kicked it just like a dog.
And when the war was over
They stuffed it just like a hog.
The spirit it was freedom and justice,
Its keepers seemed generous and kind.
Its leaders were supposed to serve the country,
But now they don't pay it no mind.
'Cause what they've been told,
It is the monster on the loose.
It's put our head into the noose,
And it just sits there watching.
They can't pay the cost,
It is a monster on the loose.
It's put our head into the noose,
And it just sits there watching.

America where are you now?
Don't you care about your sons and daughters?
Don't you know we need you now?
We can't fight alone against the monster.
But though the past has its share of injustice
Kind was the spirit in many a way
But its protectors and friends have been sleeping
and now it's a monster and will not obey.

'Cause the people grew fat and got lazy and now
their vote is a meaningless joke.
They babble about law and order,
But it's all just an echo they've been told.
The cities have turned into jungles
And corruption is strangling the land.
The police force is watching the people,
And the people just can't understand.
We don't know how to mind our own business and
The whole world has to be just like us.
Now we are fighting a war over there and no matter
who's the winner we can't pay the cost.

Frank Zappa: We get fantastic letters from anarchists, nineteen years old: "Help me in my town," and all that stuff.

Frank Kofsky: Are those the people you want to appeal to, or is that what you want people to do then—destroy the system?

Frank Zappa: No, not exactly destroy it. I want it modified to the point where it works properly. . . . First of all, the idea of busting it all down and starting all over again is stupid. The best way to do it, and what I would like to see happen, what I'm working towards, is using the system against itself to purge itself, so that it can really work. I think politics is a valid concept, but what we have today is not really politics. It's the equivalent of the high school election. It's a popularity contest. It's got nothing to do with politics—what it is is mass merchandising.

Jazz and Pop

The cry is for action and answers that will allow us to get out of this century alive.

Burt Korall

It's not a question of how the new world gets started but how the old one goes out—beautifully, gently, or with fear, hatred and bloodshed.

Arlo Guthrie

RKELEY LIBERATION
PROGRAM
Sisters and Brothers,
Unite for Survival,
Resist and Create,
Carry Out the Program,

HOW PROTEST MUSIC WORKS

Admittedly, protest music diminishes in impact once the crisis in question is past. It does, however, serve as a source of strength, unification, and expression when the battle is raging. Music's depth of importance within the civil rights movement earlier in this decade is a matter of history. It converted many to the cause in a manner that signs, demonstrations, and other means did not. Even more important, the songs solidified the chain of commitment among the followers. Northern writers, including the ever-present Pete Seegar, Phil Ochs, Tom Paxton, and Len Chandler, among others, personalized the struggle, giving their own reactions to various situations. They spoke of injustices and what had to be done. The Southern freedom singers and writers, working with the Afro-American tradition, using gospel and rhythm and blues forms and songs, with lyrics to fit each occasion, also cut deeply and made their point, leaving an enduring mark. One has only to refer back to the tremendous effect of "We Shall Overcome."

Burt Korall

WE SHALL OVERCOME

a song of West Virginia coal miners

We shall overcome, we shall overcome,
We shall overcome some day, some day;
Oh, deep in my heart, I know that I do believe
We shall overcome some day.

We shall organize, we shall organize,
We shall organize some day, some day;
Oh, deep in my heart, I know that I do believe
We shall organize some day.

We shall end Jim Crow, we shall end Jim Crow,
We shall end Jim Crow some day, some day;
Oh, deep in my heart, I know that I do believe
We shall end Jim Crow some day.

We shall walk in peace, we shall walk in peace,
We shall walk in peace some day, some day;
Oh, deep in my heart, I know that I do believe
We shall walk in peace some day.

We shall build a new world, we shall build a new world,
We shall build a new world some day, some day;
Oh, deep in my heart, I know that I do believe
We shall build a new world some day.

We'll walk hand in hand, we'll walk hand in hand,
We'll walk hand in hand some day, some day;
Oh, deep in my heart, I know that I do believe
We'll walk hand in hand some day.

We shall overcome, we shall overcome,
We shall overcome some day, some day;
Oh, deep in my heart, I know that I do believe
We shall overcome some day.

REVOLUTION is it going to be all right?

The Beatles song about revolution (1968) served as a kind of reply to the many people and songs that encourage revolution.

To those who would use violence and destruction to carry out a revolution, the Beatles said, "Count me out." To the "causes" that asked for money to support various revolutions, the Beatles said, "Wait." To those who would overthrow the "Constitution" in support of a militant communism, the Beatles recommended a mind set free.

After each reply the Beatles closed with words that sounded assuring: "It's gonna be all right." What does this mean? Were the Beatles being nostalgic and ostrich-like? Or ironic? Is the situation among people today really hopeful?

But the Beatles never had anything to do with a war. They replaced revolution with affable irreverence.

Joan Peyser

For only the men can go to the wars and bleed and die and hate; and one moment of Joe Turner singing that it's your dollar now but it's gonna be mine some sweet day is more than all they [the Beatles] have ever said. What is raw and crude in life is not for them; they are only translators.

Murray Kempton

We think it's much better to entertain people and get medals than to kill them and get medals for that.

Paul McCartney

HEAVEN opening the windows

"Heaven" presents another approach of young people today toward the world situation. At first the song seems to be encouraging a belief in an afterlife and in the protection of a divine power.

Perhaps the heaven it speaks of is associated with some central human love experience. However, this experience is not specified as romantic love; rather, it involves a looking inside and an opening of "the windows that are in your heart."

In reading the lyric one gets a feeling that the singer is an apostle of escape–maybe through drugs. Heaven is employed somehow as a symbol of a drug experience.

HEAVEN

by Felix Cavaliere

Sometimes, baby, when you're really down,
It just doesn't seem to be a ray of hope around,
And everybody that you meet kinda wears a frown,
It's cold and lonely in the heart of town.
Got to tell you all,
There, there's a place that's called heaven,
Don't you ever forget.
Now once you've heard about heaven, yeah,
I'm gonna get there yet.

Some days you laugh,
Some days you cry,
Sometimes it feels like the world passed you right by.
But everybody's got to find a peaceful place to hide.
You're out looking till you look inside,
and I see you found it.
There's a place that's called heaven.
You might think that's kinda square, oh, oh, yeah.
Don't believe in heaven,
You ain't never been there.
They try to bring you down to their way of thinking, yeah,
But don't you do it, no, no.
Don't you let it get by.
A little voice inside will tell you exactly
what you're gonna do.
Don't be blue.

Don't have to go lookin' near or far,
'Cause you can find happiness standing
right where you are.
Just open up the windows that are in your heart
And let the light shine, bring a love song
if you're really together.
There's a place that's called heaven
Filled with joy and peace, oh, oh, oh, yeah.

Once you get a look at heaven
You'll find the love that you seek.
You'll find a world filled with peace
And all your troubles will cease.
You know somebody said to keep on pushing
'Cause there's a change that's got to come.
She said thank the Lord
And every day I thank you, Lord,
For all the stars and all the seas and all the birds
and all the bees.

6 IMAGES OF the Person

One of the strongest motifs among young people today is a search for identity, a quest for self-image that is often reflected in contemporary popular song lyrics. Songs talk about "What it means to be me" or "Who am I?" They are unlike their parents and the people of earlier generations, who fostered the idea that they knew who they were. "Today's youth have no such delusions," writes Albert Goldman, "but lacking any clear-cut sense of identity has only made them more keenly aware of everyone else's."

Jerry Garcia of the Grateful Dead describes himself and his views of the world:

I wake up automatically at 9 EVERY morning (except for sometimes when I wake up later or earlier), and gaze out the window at the flocks of geese flying north/south for the winter/summer and ask myself what does it all mean? I drink as much orange juice as I can get my dirty hands on because I know that it's gonna taste good. My boots don't fit me perfectly, so my little toe hurts. Sometimes I see someone that I think I recognize, and I say hello or smile or something like that. It's fun to shoot at strangers, while they're innocently passing the house, with the sonic blaster. Especially if they're pretty, heh. Philosophically, I have nothing to say. . . . I like to play loud. . . . If I had a rocket ship or some extraterrestrial friends, you'd never see me. I hope that humanity survives the incredibly stupid hassles that we've gotten ourselves into.

Jerry Garcia

Bob Dylan, to take another example from the list of pop heroes, provides perhaps the most complex and richest study of identity and meaning in the entire folk-rock scene. "He is a continuing autobiography of this country," writes Lillian Roxon in *Rock Encyclopedia* of Dylan, "its music, its confusions, the failure of its dream."

This man, whose songs have made a whole generation of young people politically aware, came from Hibbing, Minnesota, where he lived as Robert Zimmerman and idolized Woody Guthrie.

The most important thing that can be said about Bob Dylan, and the key to a good deal of his success, is that like Jay Gatsby, he arose out of some sort of Platonic conception of himself. He created himself, which is not unusual, but he was more extreme than most of us; he created himself, name and all, from scratch, and rejected all the elements in his past except those which fit in with his carefully constructed personal mythology.

Lawrence Goldman

Bob Dylan's eyes drew you into them like whirlpools, so you had to look away to keep from being drowned in his charisma. He was sitting at an electric piano while a Japanese wind chime played random melodies on the porch outside. Dylan had owned the house for quite a while before he moved into it, a rambling American chateau of mahogany-stained shingles that clung to a mountaintop above the point where the mountaintop kept its head in the clouds. It seemed as if God and nature had joined in the conspiracy to help draw the veil of mystery and seclusion which had surrounded Dylan and his activities since he broke his neck in a motorcycle accident last year.

He wore a beard now and rimless Benjamin Franklin eyeglasses, and from behind his incognito he sang a new song he had written.

"You can change your name but you can't run away from yourself. . . . You can change your name but you can't run away from yourself . . ."

"Do you like that song?" he asked a friend.

"I think it's great," the friend said.

"I don't like that song," Dylan said.

Alfred G. Aronowitz

Today Dylan is still hurting, still searching to discover who he is. In a surprise appearance in St. Louis at a concert for The Band, Dylan was introduced as Elmer Johnson and sang four Dylan songs. Everybody else loves Dylan, but does he?

Among the beautiful people who are creating popular songs today is Joni Mitchell. Like her songs, she is simple and straightforward. In contrast to Dylan, her self-image is confident and hopeful.

And Joni, well, she's a thousand different people, and knows it; she understands everything just up to here and knows nothing at all beyond this point, which is just as it should be. She disclaims nothing, demands no credit, spends her present walking unswervingly into the future, in harmony with her world because she has accepted nothing without first understanding it and has never rejected that of herself that she did understand; what I'm getting at is she hasn't tried to choose who she is or who she will be. So she writes songs that are simple and straightforward and enormously perceptive, she makes no presumptions, she really likes people and is quite cautious—careful not to like them for the wrong reasons. In "Michael from Mountains" she really conveys how and sort of why a woman could love a man and desire a man, and that's no everyday achievement. A great many ladies have their heads so full of all they've read and heard and seen about why a man loves a woman they can think of little save how lovable they are.

Paul Williams

And from the contemporary songs themselves, different kinds of images of the person emerge. For example, some sketches of the self are optimistic and hopeful, such as "A Brand-New Me," "Early in the Morning," and "Rainy Night in Georgia." Others are pessimistic and despairing, such as "Is That All There Is,""MacArthur Park," and "The Fool on the Hill." The image of the person expressed in popular song covers a broad range of meanings, from "Cloud 9" to the indecisive "Elusive Butterfly" to the enigmatic "Suzanne." There is no one single theme or idea that links these images together. Of course, everyone wants to "be himself," but this seemingly unifying theme is deceptive, since each has a different picture of what it means to "be himself" and there are not many young people who would opt for the defiant "My Way."

In a song, a person has something about himself he wants to say, a feeling he wants to express, an experience he wants to tell others about. To understand a song lyric in the richest possible way, it should be read and discussed as a personal communication.

WHAT IS A MAN? the searching person

The author presents a list of statements which taken together seem to define "a man" for him. A man is one who stands proud, is not ashamed of his beliefs, and who can laugh and cry, love and hate, win and lose, move on or wait.

Interestingly, in each verse of the song, the answer to the question "What is a Man?" is given in the opening lines, while the closing line poses the question again. What is a man? It is as if the writer is not quite certain what his image of man is, or at least that he has not fully developed it for himself.

Some might feel that the image of man presented in the song is a rather old-fashioned one, for it speaks of winning battles and the importance of security. Others, in contrast, might feel that the image of man presented in the song contains elements of a "new generation" man. He refuses to be "phony," for example; and "he knows how to cry."

The lyric is vague enough to be open to many interpretations, depending partly on how the singer handles the words.

Perhaps what the singer really means when he asks, "What is a Man?" is more like, "If this is what a man is, what then am I?"

A BRAND-NEW ME the changed person

Popularly recorded by Dusty Springfield, this song speaks of a personal transformation of the self. The change that took place in her is such that she can sing of a "brand-new me."

Even though the physical surroundings of her life have not changed–she has the same old coat, same old shoes, same old jokes, same old grin–she is transformed within. And this has given her a whole new image of herself. She sees a brand-new girl now when she looks into the mirror.

She gives "all the credit" for this change in herself to her "boy." She has learned that one human being can really transform another in such a way that every new day of life is fresh and exciting.

MY WAY one against the world

"My Way" is a song sung by someone near the end of his life, as he looks back over his struggles.

He has a very clear and simple image of what it means to be a person. What seems to make all the pain and loss and suffering worth while is his knowledge that he did things *his way*. His words are "not the words of one who kneels."

Ironically, however, the lyrics seem to describe not the behavior of a free agent who planned "each careful step along the by-way" but of a man who had no choice but to be stoical and "hard-nosed" in the face of hardships.

Perhaps one could ask what society would be like if many people cultivated in their own lives the attitudes of the man described in "My Way."

MY WAY

by Paul Anka, J. Revaux, C. Francois

And now the end is near
And so I face the final curtain.
My friend, I'll say it clear.
I'll state my case of which I'm certain.
I've lived a life that's full.
I traveled each and every highway.
And more, much more than this,
I did it my way.
Regrets, I've had a few
But then again, too few to mention.
I did what I had to do
And saw it thru without exemption.
I planned each chartered course,
Each careful step along the by-way.
And more, much more than this
I did it my way.

Yes, there were times I'm sure you knew
When I bit off more than I could chew.
But thru it all when there was doubt
I ate it up, and spit it out.
I faced it all and I stood tall
And did it my way.

I've loved, I've laughed and cried
I've had my fill, my share of losing.
And now, as tears subside,
I find it all so amusing.
To think I did all that, and may I say,
"Not in a shy way."
Oh, no, oh, no, not me;
I did it my way.

For what is a man, what has he got if not himself.
Then he has got to say the things he truly feels
And not the words of one who kneels.
The record shows I took the blows and did it my way.

IS THAT ALL THERE IS? **the hopeless person**

The story of the girl described in this lyric is a story of a series of disappointments. "Is that all there is?" she repeats time and again throughout her life. She expected security as a child–loving parents and a home–and it was wiped out by fire. She found something "missing" even in the circus, the greatest show on earth, which had been one of the most exciting events of her childhood. Her time of being in love was cut short, and long love-walks together by the river stopped happening when her "most wonderful boy in the world" suddenly left her. "Is that all there is?" she asks again. Even death or suicide, she feels, would probably be a disappointment to her. The only thing left in life, then, is to dance and drink with her friends of the moment.

THE FOOL ON THE HILL the rejected person

A very different kind of human being is described in this surrealistic Beatle song. He is the Fool on the Hill. Day after day he stands motionless on the hill wearing a foolish grin.

He is indeed a strange creature, and most people seem to want to avoid him. The Beatles at least are fascinated enough with the Fool to tell others about him.

The Fool seems to feel no need to apologize for himself or to give an answer. He has a "thousand voices" and doubtless much to tell the world, but no one ever hears him. He doesn't notice their unconcern, instead he keeps talking "perfectly loud."

Many who listen to this song apparently find it easy to identify themselves with the Fool on the Hill, feeling that in the eyes of the world they are foolish and their ideas worthless. But they may also think that like him they have some kind of message for "the world spinning round," even though nobody listens.

RAINY NIGHT IN GEORGIA a man found all over the world

The story here is of a musician who is a victim of circumstances. Trying to do his "own thing," he finds himself lonely and cold. Every sound he hears, everything he sees—especially the rain, the lights and noises of the city at night—seem to echo his feelings of sadness.

In this situation, the best he can hope for is comfort in knowing there is someone who loves him, who reassures him: "It's all right."

There is nothing in this lyric of the defiance of "My Way," or the exuberance of "A Brand-New Me." But perhaps among all the songs it is the one with which most young people empathize, especially those who are searching for identity and meaning.

EARLY IN THE MORNING

the ordinary person

Very close in some ways to the mid-century American popular song tradition, the song contrasts the feelings that come to the singer at night, when there is nothing much to see or do, with the good feelings he experiences in the brightness of the morning, when there is a new sun shining on the meadow and songbirds in the willow trees.

The song reflects a simple concept of life. Images of good feeling are associated with the simple things of nature: meadows, weeping willows, songbirds. Yet, also, there is complexity here. The morning tells him that there is a someone "coming home." We don't know who this someone is, and just when the someone will be coming home is kept vague. We also wonder where this someone has been, and whether there is any significance in the differences between the final phrases of each verse, *i.e.*, "coming home, home to me" and "coming home, home with me."

MacARTHUR PARK the wondering man

Jimmy Webb's lyric describes a man of intense feelings and passion. For him a lifetime of experiences and plans seems to swirl in his mind now in a confusion of images.

Perhaps MacArthur Park is a place where he came to a realization. Perhaps the cake is a symbol of a love relationship that has come and gone. He looks forward to "another song" and further "loves" but he will never rest from "wondering why" this one relationship didn't work out.

MacARTHUR PARK

by Jimmy Webb

Spring has never waited for us, girl,
It ran one step ahead as we followed in a dance
Between the parted pages
And were pressed in love's hot fevered iron
Like a stripped pair of pants.

MacArthur Park is melting in the dark,
All the sweet, green icing flowing down,
Someone left the cake out in the rain.
I don't think that I can make it,
'Cause it took so long to bake it,
And I'll never have the recipe again, oh, no.
I recall the yellow cotton dress foaming like a wave
on the ground around your knees,
The birds like tender babies in your hands,
And the old men playing checkers by the trees.

(Repeat chorus).

There will be another song for me, for I will sing it,
There will be another dream for me,
Someone will bring it.
I will drink the wine while it is warm
And never let you catch me looking at the sun,
But after all the loves of my life,
After all the loves of my life,
You'll still be the one.
I will take my life into my hands
And I will use it.
I will win the worship in their eyes
And I will lose it.
I will have the things that I desire
And my passion flow like rivers to the sky.
But after all the loves of my life,
Oh, after all the loves of my life,
I'll be thinking of you, and wondering why.

(Repeat chorus).

ELUSIVE BUTTERFLY the love-seeker

Like many other contemporary writers, Bob Lind seeks to define the indefinable. He succeeds very well in communicating his constant search and subtly invites love while seemingly only chasing its elusive form.

ELUSIVE BUTTERFLY

by Bob Lind

You might wake up some morning,
To the sound of something moving
Past your window in the wind.
And if you're quick enough to rise,
You'll catch the fleeting glimpse
Of someone's fading shadow.

Don't be concerned, it will not harm you.
It's only me pursuing something I'm not sure of.
Across my dream, with nets of wonder,
I chase the bright elusive butterfly of love.

Out on the new horizon,
You may see the floating motion
Of a distant pair of wings.
And if the sleep has left your ears,
You might hear footsteps
Running through an open meadow.

You might have heard my footsteps
Echo softly in the distance
Through the canyons of your mind.
I might have even called your name
As I ran searching after
Something to believe in.

Don't be concerned, it will not harm you.
It's only me pursuing something I'm not sure of.
Across my dream, with nets of wonder,
I chase the bright elusive butterfly of love.

You might have seen me running
Through the long abandoned ruins
Of the dreams you left behind.
If you remember something there
That glided past you followed
Close by heavy breathing,

Don't be concerned, it will not harm you.
It's only me pursuing something I'm not sure of.
Across my dream, with nets of wonder,
I chase the bright elusive butterfly of love.

SUZANNE unique woman, unique situation

In an age of concern about the image of woman, popular music has many things to say. In the early days of rock music, there were simply two kinds of women. One was the *goddess,* whom Richard Goldstein describes as the one whom "you dreamed about and blamed your acne on." The second was the *girl friend,* the one whom the boy danced with and tried unsuccessfully to "make." The women in the early days of rock music were mostly objects of worship or desire.

Today, it is difficult to categorize the women who appear in popular songs. It is impossible to describe them according to any society's norms. In the main, each woman is a unique, unclassifiable reality.

Leonard Cohen's "Suzanne" is a woman who is a mixture of maiden, temptress, teacher, and lover. She seems half crazy, and yet she seems to have the wisdom of a madonna. She is a paradox of weakness and power, of wretchedness and grandeur; she is feline, yet evocative of a supernatural, superhuman Jesus. She is the untouchable whom you have touched, yet in the end she seems to be very strong for you because she's totally in touch with herself–her body somehow at one with her mind.

No other woman in any song is like this woman. Her situation is specific, never to be duplicated, unique; and so it is with other great songs about woman in contemporary musical literature.

SUZANNE

by Leonard Cohen

Suzanne takes you down
To her place near the river.
You can hear the boats go by,
You can stay the night beside her,
And you know that she's half-crazy
But that's why you want to be there,
And she feeds you tea and oranges
That come all the way from China,
And just when you mean to tell her
That you have no love to give her,
Then she gets you on her wave-length
And she lets the river answer
That you've always been her lover.

And you want to travel with her,
And you want to travel blind,
And you know that she can trust you
'Cause you've touched her perfect body
With your mind.

And Jesus was a sailor
When he walked upon the water
And he spent a long time watching
From a lonely wooden tower
And when he knew for certain
That only drowning men could see him,
He said, "All men shall be sailors, then,
Until the sea shall free them,"

But he, himself, was broken
Long before the sky would open.
Forsaken, almost human,
He sank beneath your wisdom
Like a stone.

And you want to travel with him,
And you want to travel blind,
And you think you'll maybe trust him
'Cause he touched your perfect body
With his mind.

Suzanne takes your hand
And she leads you to the river.
She is wearing rags and feathers
From Salvation Army counters,
And the sun pours down like honey
On our lady of the harbor;
And she shows you where to look
Among the garbage and the flowers.
There are heroes in the seaweed,
There are children in the morning,
They are leaning out for love,
And they will lean that way forever
While Suzanne, she holds the mirror.

And you want to travel with her,
You want to travel blind,
And you're sure that she can find you
'Cause she's touched her perfect body
With her mind.